EAST

Also by Meera Sodha

Made in India
Fresh India

MEERA SODHA
EAST

120 Vegan and Vegetarian Recipes
from Bangalore to Beijing

Photography by **David Loftus**
Art Direction by **John Hamilton**
Illustrations by **Monika Forsberg**

FLATIRON
BOOKS
NEW YORK

For John Hamilton (1963–2019)
I feel so lucky that our paths crossed

contents:

ALTERNATIVE CONTENTS

V: VEGAN
VO: VEGAN OPTION

Spring

Asparagus and snow peas with chile peanut crumbs (V)	58
Peanut butter and broccolini pad thai (V)	78
Thai green curry with eggplant, zucchini, and snow peas (V)	120
Spring pilau with asparagus, fennel, and pea (V)	139

Summer

Chargrilled summer vegetables with a dhana-jeera dressing (V)	50
Sri Lankan beet curry with green bean mallum (V)	100
Tomato curry (V)	108
Tomato, pistachio, and saffron tart (VO)	194

Autumn

Squash malai kari (V)	107
Eggplant pollichattu (V)	118
Autumn pilau with squash, lacinato kale, and smoked garlic (V)	143
Celery root, tofu, and kale gado gado (V)	172

Winter

Rutabaga laksa (V)	74
Shiitake pho with crispy leeks (V)	87
Udon noodles with red cabbage and cauliflower (V)	88
Brussels sprout nasi goreng (V)	132

INTRODUCTION

Life can change in an instant, like mine did with a phone call.

That's how I felt when Melissa Denes, an editor at the *Guardian*, called me. She said they were introducing a new vegan column into the weekend magazine and she wanted me to write it. In my most private moments I had dared to dream about writing a column, but I never seriously thought it would happen. As I weighed up the options, I realized there were a few small problems.

For a start, I wasn't vegan.

Secondly, up until that point, I had only written about Indian food.

Thirdly, I'd just had a baby who was a few weeks old. Not only had life just been thrown into chaos with her arrival, but I'd planned to take a whole year off to get to know her.

This was an amazing opportunity that had come at the worst possible time. I had every reason to say no, but I said yes.

I was excited to enter this brave new world in which I found myself. Huge numbers of people, growing by the day, were choosing to eat a more plant-based diet, whether for political, environmental, ethical, or economic reasons. Although a relatively small number were actually becoming vegan, a larger number were looking to reduce the amount of meat and dairy in their diet. This felt like a big and important discussion—I wanted a chance to be a part of it and help move the conversation forward.

At that time, many of the recipes being touted for vegans weren't tempting. They didn't make me hungry. Plant-based food was either still in the shadows of its association with granola-munching hippies or hijacked by healthy eating. It felt as though the pleasures of eating and the importance of flavor had been forgotten.

As an outsider, I thought I was in a good place to create new and exciting vegan recipes. I understood meat-eaters and knew the textures, flavors, and the "richness" they might miss. But I had also spent two years writing a vegetarian book, *Fresh India*, and knew how to make bitter kale leaves sing and how to tempt a beet hater into eating a plateful.

I signed the contract with the *Guardian* and so began my journey. It started with some difficult first weeks, but winter turned to spring and suddenly two years had passed. I learned many things along the way.

I was stuck for new recipes to begin with, but I suspected that by looking beyond India to East Asia and South East Asia I would find further inspiration for how to shift vegetables from the side to the center of the table. I had already traveled to Sri Lanka and eaten sublime beet and cashew curries. In Thailand, I had memorized every twist in the plot of som tam salad and counted down the minutes between meals until my next pad thai. I had been soothed inside out by many a congee in London's Chinatown and had my tastebuds electrified with bowlfuls of dan dan noodles. I was hungry for more.

I also found vegan constraints are a catalyst for creativity. Not cooking with meat, fish, dairy, or eggs forced me to think in new and interesting ways. I discovered the wonderful world of the Asian pantry: fermented, pickled, and salted ingredients—things like kimchi, sweet miso, and gochujang, all of which add flavor to a meal in an instant.

Veganism wasn't my only constraint. I had much less time on my hands too now that I was a new mum. This meant that elaborate dishes, or those that required too much time to prepare or cook, were left by the wayside. They didn't make the cut into my column, or into this book.

The biggest limitation of all was not being able to travel to the countries whose food I wanted to explore further. When writing my Indian cookbooks, I had traveled for months at a time, taking sharp turns when someone recommended a

new dish, or a cook I had to meet. But Arya was still so young and dependent on me, and I didn't want to leave her. This time, I traveled by reading: I followed Fuchsia Dunlop around the streets of Chengdu and saw 1990s Jakarta through Madhur Jaffrey's eyes.

When I ran out of books, I packed baby Arya and a notebook into a little baby carrier and off we went on a food safari to find the best laksa, bun cha, or massaman curry in London.

I found that I could travel to Asia without traveling very far at all. I spoke to my accountant, Ben, who is from Borneo, where Sarawak laksa is prized. I begged Wichet, the owner-chef of the Thai restaurant Supawan, to show me how to make a tom kha ghai soup, and Shuko Oda, the Japanese chef, to teach me how to make her walnut miso. I accosted home cooks on social media who had innocently posted photos of their breakfast to ask them more about what they ate and how they made it.

Two years later, the time felt right to bring all these recipes together in a book. Some are vegetarian, not vegan, because this is, in the main, how I like to eat—and therefore not all of them have featured in my column.

This isn't an attempt to be an authoritative voice on Asian food: to undertake such a survey would take years. This is food I've created in my kitchen based on a very personal journey and an adventure. And this is now how I like to cook for my family and friends, and for myself. It is the food I've come to love—and I hope you love it too.

As I finish writing this book, Arya is a toddler and starting to piece her first words together. I've felt so much guilt along the way and I am sure this tension between work, life, and motherhood will always be present. But if there's one lesson that I wanted to teach my daughter from the moment I met her, it is this: she should dream. Sometimes what she dares to dream won't be easy to achieve, but it'll be worth it in the end.

ABOUT THIS BOOK

Principally, I have written this book because I love vegetables and want to help you to eat more of them—it's therefore intended to be a very practical book. For that reason it's deliberately structured by the types of meals you will find across South, East, and South East Asia, i.e. noodles, rice, and curries. There may have been more poetic ways to structure it, but I wanted to help you find your heart's desire quickly, so that you're able to get on with the joyful business of cooking, eating, and spending time with your family and friends.

Many of the recipes I originally wrote for the *Guardian* over the last two years are published here in this book. I've tried not to tinker with them too much, but where a recipe could have been made simpler without destroying its soul, I have simplified it.

Most of the recipes are based on foods native to particular cuisines which I have eaten in a home or restaurant and then tinkered with to make my own. Others are adaptations of recipes from home cooks or other food writers (who are credited within the recipe). I don't claim that anything in the book is authentic to anywhere, other than myself, but where I have used the name of a dish of a particular community—for example the Korean bibimbap—I've tried my best to stick as closely to either the ingredients that identify that dish and/or cooking technique as possible.

The recipes in this book are by and large speedy enough to make during the week and with ingredients you can most likely find in your local supermarket. When it comes to ingredients, when you start with the best, life becomes simple. I didn't always feel this way, especially not after watching home cooks in Dharavi, India's biggest slum, transform some very old, bendy vegetables into delicious meals. But what I now know to be true is that the more delicious the raw ingredient, the less you have to do to it.

It is also true that we are all, as George Orwell said in *The Road to Wigan Pier*, "primarily a bag for putting food into; the other functions and faculties may be more godlike, but in point of time they come afterwards." Considering we all have only one bag, we ought to treat it with the utmost care.

To me, "best" means produce grown by good people in good ways: unfussed with, largely chemical-free, locally, and in season. And where produce involves animals (dairy and eggs), those animals must be happy and well looked after, meaning "free range," "organic," and "higher welfare." But "best" may mean something different to you.

As for the Asian pantry ingredients, many are salted, pickled, or fermented, such as soy sauce—the techniques and time for which are beyond the means of most home cooks. Embrace this, it's not cheating—but buy the best products you can and always check the labels to see if they're suitable for vegans or vegetarians.

Many can be bought in supermarkets in the broadly named "ethnic aisle," or in Indian or East Asian supermarkets, or online (a list of suppliers is on page 293). I would urge you to find your local Indian or East Asian shop and buy from there—not least because these places are like Aladdin's caves, filled with unimaginable treasure, but also because you can pick up really good-quality, fresh, and cheap ingredients such as silken tofu, bunches of basil, and fresh kimchi.

With regard to equipment, I think you'll have most things you'll need in your kitchen to cook these recipes. The tools I have found most helpful in making the recipes in this book are: a sharp knife; a 12-inch non-stick deep-sided frying pan with a tight-fitting clear lid (to see what's cooking); a garlic press; and a julienne peeler that can transform vegetables into long thin noodles perfect for salads. Every recipe has been written using standardized measuring spoons and cups and a set of digital scales. Scales aren't always necessary, but they are helpful in baking recipes, where precision is key, and they will also help to develop your intuition, which can make for a more freestyle way of cooking when you gain your kitchen confidence.

And finally, on building confidence, I want to leave you with the advice my mother gave me when I first started cooking with her—and which still remains the best piece of advice anyone has ever given me: "Taste your ingredients before, during, and after cooking—that way you'll understand how they behave."

KEY

In the recipes, "V" is for "vegan" and "VO" is for "vegan option" (the option is clearly indicated in the ingredients or recipe note). All unmarked recipes are suitable for vegetarians.

Many recipes can be made gluten-free or suitable for people with celiac disease simply by substituting the soy sauce with tamari.

snacks & small things

There are those who righteously stand up for breakfast as the most important meal of the day and those who tout the benefits of family dinners (and I'm not denying either). But where is the ambassador for snacking? If the position is vacant, I'll happily apply.

In my opinion, a life well lived is a life full of small edible delights: little opportunities of deliciousness that can be woven into a day. Sadly, in much of Europe and America, we've become a bit too hooked on very convenient but highly processed and sugary snacks—the sort that are mass-produced and presented in uniform packages in our convenience stores and supermarkets. But in Asia, for the most part, things are different and freshness and variety reign supreme.

In Bangkok, a snack might be a freshly pounded salad: the rising smell of lemongrass, mixing with chile and garlic, catching on the midday heat and sending your taste buds into overdrive. In Darjeeling, you might polish off a plate of momos (see page 34): perfectly sized little dumplings with a big bang of flavor, dipped into chile sauce. You might float down the Mekong River while chomping your way through a sizzling rice-flour crêpe (see page 197), doused in the famous sweet-and-sour Vietnamese sauce, nuoc cham.

At their best, snacks like these can be the best thing you'll eat all day: artfully made by masters of their craft—and not just the filler between more important meals. They can be enjoyed when you're on your own—standing up at a night market, or sitting on a train platform—or with a group of friends. When it comes to snacking, there are no rules.

Of course, everyone is anti-snacking these days for health reasons, but snacks don't have to be unhealthy, especially if you make them yourself. I hope this chapter will inspire you to think a little more about those in-between moments, and make the most of them.

MUSHROOM BAO

There is genuine pleasure to be had in things that feel just right: the weight of a pound coin, a bath at the perfect temperature, the feel of a well-worn wooden spoon. To this list, I'd add the bao: this little bun, a staple of Taiwanese street-food stalls, is ergonomically designed for eating—it fits snugly into the nook of a hand; the pillowy dough gives like memory foam; and the semicircular shape slots cleanly into the mouth.

note / You'll need a steamer: the inexpensive bamboo ones are brilliant.

Makes: 10 bao /

For the bao buns /

3 cups + 2 tbsp all-purpose flour,
  plus extra for dusting

1 tsp instant yeast

2 tbsp sugar

½ tsp salt

1¼ tsp baking powder

1 cup warm water

canola oil

For the pickled cucumber /

⅓ cup rice vinegar

½ a cucumber, halved, deseeded,
  and thinly sliced

For the mushroom filling /

⅓ cup soy sauce

¼ cup creamy peanut butter

2½ tbsp rice vinegar

4 cloves of garlic, crushed

4 tsp toasted sesame oil

2 tbsp canola oil

1½ lbs oyster and shiitake
  mushrooms, thinly sliced

a handful of salted peanuts, ground
  or finely chopped

Start by making the dough. Combine the dry ingredients in a bowl, then add the water little by little and bring the dough together using your hands; you should have a sticky ball. Turn it out onto a floured surface and knead for 5 minutes, until smooth and bouncy, then place in an oiled bowl. Cover with a kitchen towel and leave in a warm place to double in size for 1 to 1½ hours.

Meanwhile, put the vinegar for the pickled cucumber into a small saucepan with 3 tablespoons of water. Bring to a simmer, then pour into a bowl, add the cucumber, and leave to cool.

Turn the dough out onto a floured surface, knead for a minute to knock out the air, then divide into 10 equal pieces. Take one piece, flatten it into a ½-inch-thick disk, then brush one half with a little oil. Fold the bun into a half-moon and place on a small square of parchment paper on a tray. Repeat with the remaining dough, then loosely cover the tray with a kitchen towel and leave to rise for 30 minutes more.

Now for the filling. In a small bowl, whisk the soy sauce, peanut butter, vinegar, garlic, and sesame oil. Heat the canola oil in a frying pan on a high flame, then fry the mushrooms for 6 minutes, until soft and browning at the edges. Stir in the sauce to coat, then turn the heat to medium and cook, stirring regularly, for 5 minutes, until the sauce reduces and darkens.

To cook the bao, set a steamer over a pan of simmering water. Put the bao, still on their parchment-paper mats, into the steamer in batches, making sure they don't touch. Cover and steam for 8 minutes.

Once done, fill each bao with a generous tablespoon of mushrooms, 3 or 4 slices of cucumber and, for a little crunch, some peanuts.

SWEET POTATO CAKES
with kimchi mayo

One of the unspoken rules of cooking is that two sweet ingredients (like sweet potato and corn) shouldn't go together. They are apparently too sweet to complement each other. I disagree. In these savory cakes they provide the perfect backing track on which the heat of the fresh green chile and the sour creaminess of the mayo can sing.

note / Check the label of the kimchi to make sure it's suitable for vegans. You'll need a food processor or immersion blender for this recipe.

Serves 4 /

For the sweet potato cakes /

1 lb sweet potatoes (2 medium)

1 green finger (or serrano) chile, very finely chopped

⅓ of an 11 oz can of corn, drained

a handful of fresh cilantro, chopped, plus extra to serve

½ tsp salt

1 fat clove of garlic, crushed

3 green onions, finely sliced

canola oil, to fry

For the kimchi mayo /

¼ cup packed chopped kimchi

½ cup mayonnaise (or vegan mayo—see page 255)

Preheat the oven to 400°F.

Peel the sweet potatoes and cut into 1-inch-thick chunks, then place on a sheet pan and bake for 25 to 30 minutes until tender and a knife slips through them easily. Leave them to cool, then place in a bowl and mash with a fork until smooth.

Meanwhile, make the kimchi mayo by blending the kimchi and mayonnaise together, either in the small bowl of a food processor or using an immersion blender. Scrape into a serving bowl and leave to one side.

To make the cakes, add the chile, corn, cilantro, salt, garlic, and green onions to the mashed sweet potato and mix very well with your hands. Bring together into a ball. Cut the ball in half, then cut each half into 4 pieces so you have 8 equal pieces. Take a piece, roll between your palms to form a ball, then flatten into a round patty around ½-in thick. Place on a plate, then shape the rest.

To cook the cakes, heat a teaspoon of oil in a large non-stick frying pan over a medium-high heat. When hot, add 4 cakes (or as many as you're able to fit) to the pan and fry for 5 minutes, turning halfway through, or when lovely and golden on each side. (You can keep them warm on a plate in the oven at 250°F.)

When you're ready to eat, place a couple of cakes on each plate, sprinkle with cilantro, and serve with kimchi mayo.

ONIGIRI stuffed with walnut miso   V

Onigiri are Japanese rice balls, made with sushi rice and often filled with pickles. They are the perfect portable snack. In the seventeenth century, Japanese samurai stored rice balls wrapped in bamboo to have as a quick lunch during war. Mine are stuffed with my variation on Shuko Oda's sweet, rich walnut miso, from her restaurant Koya in Soho, London.

note / If you don't have white miso, double the quantity of brown rice miso. You'll need a blender or food processor for this recipe.

Makes 8 onigiri /

2 cups sushi rice
2 sheets of nori

For the walnut miso /
1 cup walnuts
1 tbsp brown rice miso
1 tbsp white miso
2½ tbsp agave syrup
1 tsp rice vinegar

Preheat the oven to 400°F.

Place the rice in a medium-sized lidded saucepan and cover with lukewarm water. Agitate with your hand until the water turns cloudy. Drain and repeat, until the water runs clear, then cover with warm water and leave to soak for 5 minutes. Drain the rice, then tip back into the saucepan and add scant 2 cups of cold water. Place the pan over a high heat with the lid on, bring to the boil, then immediately turn the heat down to a whisper and cook for 10 minutes. Take off the heat and leave to steam with the lid on for a further 10 minutes.

While the rice is steaming, place your walnuts on a baking sheet and toast in the oven for 6 minutes, or until starting to turn golden. Remove and allow to cool. Put both misos into a blender or food processor and add the agave syrup and vinegar, then pulse to combine. Add the roasted walnuts and pulse a few more times until you have a chunky paste.

Now you are ready to shape the onigiri. Prepare your nori by cutting it into strips 1 inch wide. You will also need a clean board and a bowl of water large enough to rinse your hands. With wet hands, take ¾ cup of the cooked sushi rice and form it into a ball. With your thumb, make a deep indent in the center. Take ½ tablespoon of the walnut filling and drop it into the indent. Shape the rice up and over the miso filling and squeeze into a dense ball. Place this in the middle of a strip of nori, and bring the nori up around the onigiri so that it looks as if it is wearing a belt. Repeat with the remaining rice and miso, leaving you with 8 belted chubby onigiri ready for your lunch.

CHILE SALT PINEAPPLE

Galle Face is a stretch of promenade in Colombo, Sri Lanka, where the land dissolves into sea and where, at sunset, the hungry go to feast on an array of colorful snacks. This sweet, sour, and hot pineapple is one of them—not so much a recipe as a way to enjoy the fruit. The ratios of salt, sugar, and chile are just how I like them, but feel free to play around until it tastes just right to you. Best served at home alongside an arrack sour, or a gin and tonic.

Serves a small crowd /

1 medium pineapple

1 tsp salt

2 tsp sugar

1 tsp red chile powder, such as Kashmiri

1 tbsp lime juice (from 1 lime)

Cut the top and bottom off the pineapple and stand it upright. Using a sharp knife, carefully peel the skin off the pineapple by skirting the knife close to the flesh all the way around. Place on its side and nick any brown spikes out of the flesh using the tip of a small knife. Cut the pineapple lengthways into 8 pieces, removing the tough core from each wedge. Cut each wedge into ½-inch slices.

Mix the salt, sugar, and chile powder in a small pretty bowl. Serve this next to the wedges on a bigger platter. Just before serving, sprinkle the pineapple wedges with lime juice and encourage people to dip the wedges into the chile salt with their hands.

CELERY AND PEANUT WONTONS
with chile soy sauce

Move over wood ear mushrooms, there's a new wonton filling in town: celery and peanuts. Usually these two ingredients are found together in refreshing crunchy salads on Chinese tables, but here they are cooked together to form a comfortingly delicious, sweet, and sophisticated dish. This is unbelievably easy to make, given that the wonton wrappers—which I keep on hand in the freezer—just need to be pressed shut around the filling and the sauce is largely made up of pantry ingredients.

note / Wonton wrappers can be found in larger or Asian supermarkets. You'll need a food processor for this recipe.

Makes 24 wontons (serves 4–6) /

For the wontons /
1½ cups unsalted peanuts
2 lbs celery
¼ cup canola oil
4 cloves of garlic, crushed
2 tbsp soy sauce
24 wonton wrappers (or egg-free gyoza wrappers, if vegan), defrosted

For the chile soy sauce /
2 tbsp canola oil
1 tbsp toasted sesame oil
¼ cup soy sauce
2 cloves of garlic, crushed
1 tsp chile flakes
1½ tbsp white wine vinegar
2 green onions, chopped

First, make the wonton filling. Place the peanuts in a food processor and blitz into crumble. Roughly chop the celery, setting aside some leaves to garnish the dish, then place in the food processor with the peanut crumble. Pulse until the pieces resemble coarse ground meat. Heat the canola oil in a pan and, when hot, add the celery and peanut mixture. Cook for 15 to 20 minutes over a medium heat, stirring frequently to remove as much water as possible, then add the garlic and soy sauce and cook for a further 5 minutes. Take off the heat and leave to one side to cool.

To make the chile soy sauce, place all the ingredients in a saucepan. Bring to the boil, then immediately take off the heat.

To fill the wontons, lay a wrapper in front of you in a diamond shape. Put 1½ teaspoons of filling into the center. Brush the edges of the wonton lightly with water and fold in half to form a triangle. Press down around the filling (to make sure there are no air bubbles), then press outwards to seal it properly and place on a plate. Repeat.

To cook the wontons, drop in batches (of around 6) into a pan of boiling water for 5 minutes at a time, then drain. To serve, divide the wontons between your plates, drizzle some of the sauce over each portion, then scatter over the celery leaves.

See photos overleaf

**CELERY AND PEANUT WONTONS
WITH CHILE SOY SAUCE**

MUM'S BEET AND GINGER SOUP   VO

This is one of a handful of soups my mother has been making for years. I didn't include it in my first book, *Made in India*, because it didn't feel very "Indian," but family recipes are messy, eclectic, and wonderful things, forged over many years, that don't often fit into neat categories. When writing this recipe down, I asked Mum how much ginger to add. She said, "According to the weather," so the quantity given here is for a cold winter's day. By all means kick it up a notch for extra warmth.

note / This soup goes well with a chunk of grilled sourdough bread and thick tart yogurt seasoned with a pinch of salt. Make sure the vegetable stock is suitable for vegans if you're a vegan.

Serves 4 /

3 tbsp canola oil

1 medium onion, chopped

¾ inch ginger, peeled and grated

3 cloves of garlic, crushed

1 green finger (or serrano) chile, finely chopped

1 lb raw beets, scrubbed and grated

¼ lb potato (1 small), peeled and grated

3 cups vegan vegetable stock

salt, to taste

thick yogurt, non-dairy if vegan, nigella seeds, and grilled sourdough, to serve

Heat the oil in a large saucepan and, once it's good and hot, add the onion and fry for 10 minutes, stirring occasionally. Add the ginger, garlic, and chile, then fry for 3 minutes, stirring all the while. Add the beet and potato, stir to coat, then pour in the stock and bring to the boil. Turn down the heat and leave to simmer for 30 minutes.

Leave the soup to cool a little, then blend and taste—add up to ¼ teaspoon of salt if you like. Transfer the soup into bowls and top with a spoonful of yogurt and a sprinkling of nigella seeds. Serve hot with the grilled sourdough.

POTATO DOSA with pea and coconut chutney

V

"Have you eaten the potato dosa?" Rhea asked me while we cooked in her kitchen in Mumbai. "It's grated potato which is pressed and pan-fried like a dosa." Sounds a lot like a rösti, I thought, and perhaps that was its origin given that ideas can potentially travel 4,111 miles from Bern (the Swiss capital, where rösti originated) to Mumbai in a nanosecond via the Internet. In any case, here it identifies as a dosa, and is accompanied by a delicious pea and coconut chutney.

note / You'll need a food processor for this recipe.

Makes 4 /

⅓ cup dried shredded coconut

1½ cups frozen peas, defrosted, plus a handful to serve

1 clove of garlic, chopped

1 tbsp lime juice (from 1 lime)

2 green finger (or serrano) chiles, chopped

salt

1½ lbs (2 medium) Russet potatoes

½ a medium red onion, very finely chopped

8 fresh curry leaves, shredded, plus 6 more to serve

½ inch ginger, peeled and grated

½ tsp cumin seeds

¼ tsp ground black pepper

canola oil

To make the pea and coconut chutney, place the shredded coconut in a small heatproof bowl, pour ⅓ cup of just-boiled water over it, and leave for 5 minutes. Transfer the coconut and water to a food processor, add the peas, garlic, lime juice, ½ a green chile, and ½ a teaspoon of salt, and blend until smooth. Scrape into a little bowl and leave to one side.

To make the dosas, peel and coarsely grate the potatoes. Put them into a clean kitchen towel and twist hard, over a sink, to squeeze out as much water as possible. Put the potatoes into a large bowl and add the onion, the 8 shredded curry leaves, the remaining 1½ green chiles, ginger, cumin seeds, black pepper, and ½ a teaspoon of salt. Mix, mix, mix with your hands until everything is well distributed.

Heat ½ tablespoon of oil in a frying pan over a low flame. Take a quarter of the mixture and form it into a rough round (don't worry if it's a bit juicy: it will stick together in the pan). Place in the pan and gently press with the back of a tablespoon to flatten it. Cook for around 5 minutes, then carefully flip over using a spatula, and cook for another 5 minutes, until crispy and brown. Remove to a plate—keep warm by covering with foil—and repeat with the remaining mixture.

Just before serving, drizzle a little oil into the pan while it's still hot and add the 6 whole curry leaves. Wait until the leaves crackle, then place it all on the chutney along with a handful of peas. To serve, stack the dosas on a plate with the chutney alongside.

snacks & small things

SWEET POTATO MOMOS

V

I ate my first momo in Darjeeling, at a stall run by an elderly Nepalese lady. As I waited, she filled and pleated a dozen with machine-like efficiency. I had low expectations, as the filling was a mix of white cabbage and carrot (neither is known for its striking personality)—but a torrent of flavor ripped through the first bite, and I returned to her stall many times to learn her secret. In this recipe I have filled them with sweet potato, but feel free to tinker with the filling: mushroom and tofu are good alternatives. The pleating might look daunting but momos can be pressed shut by toddlers without too much damage to aesthetics.

note / Dumpling wrappers are sometimes called "gyoza dumpling wrappers" or "dumpling pastry," and can be bought in an Asian supermarket and kept in the freezer. Check the packaging carefully as some dumpling wrappers contain egg.

Makes 22–25 momos /

For the sauce /
2 tbsp toasted sesame oil
¼ cup dark soy sauce
2 tsp sugar
1½ tbsp white wine vinegar
1 tsp chile flakes

For the dumplings /
canola oil
2 cloves of garlic, crushed
1 bird's-eye chile, finely chopped
1 lb sweet potatoes (2 medium),
  peeled and grated
2 tsp dark soy sauce
½ tsp salt
4 green onions, very finely sliced
25 dumpling wrappers, defrosted

To make the sauce, simply whisk all the ingredients together in a small bowl and set aside until you serve.

For the filling, heat 2 tablespoons of oil in a frying pan and, when hot, add the garlic and chile and sizzle for a minute, until it smells fragrant. Add the sweet potatoes, stir-fry for a minute, then add the soy sauce and salt, and cook for 3 minutes more, until there's no liquid left in the pan. Off the heat, fold in the sliced green onions and leave to cool a little.

To make up the dumplings, lay out a large plate or chopping board and fill a little bowl with water. Take one wrapper (cover the rest with a damp kitchen towel to stop them drying out) and put a tablespoon of the filling mixture in its center. Wet a finger and use it to dampen the exposed parts of the wrapper, then fold over to enclose the filling, and pinch and pleat the wrapper closed, working from one side to the other and pressing out as much air as possible.

To cook the dumplings, heat a tablespoon of oil in a saucepan on a low flame. When hot, add as many momos as can comfortably fit in a single layer, and fry for 2 minutes, until the bottoms are golden. Then add 5 tablespoons of water and cover the pan with a lid. Leave to steam for 6 to 7 minutes, or until the pastry is soft and the water has evaporated, and serve hot with the dipping sauce on the side.

OVERNIGHT SOY EGGS

These eggs should really be squirreled away in the condiments section, but I thought they might get lost in there. They are perfectly seasoned and hugely versatile mouthfuls of joy. Since discovering them, I now eat them in the morning on toast with quickly fried greens, during the day on their own, and in the evening to top ramen (see page 92) or congee. I soft-boil a batch of eggs in the evening until just jammy, throw them into the marinade, and they're ready to use the next day and the whole of the following week.

Makes 6 eggs /

¼ cup + 3 tbsp soy sauce
1 tbsp white wine vinegar
2 tbsp superfine sugar
6 large eggs

First, set up somewhere to leave your eggs to marinate. I like to use a Kilner jar, but you could also use a deep plastic box. Pour the soy sauce, vinegar, sugar, and ⅔ cup of cold water into your chosen container and stir to mix.

Next, take a bowl that will fit all the eggs and put a couple of handfuls of ice inside. Pour cold water into the bowl so that it's three-quarters full, and leave to one side.

To cook the eggs, take a saucepan just big enough to hold the eggs snugly (so they can't rattle around too much), fill it half full of water, and bring to the boil over a medium-high heat. When the water is at a rolling boil, gently lower the eggs into the water using a large spoon. Cook for exactly 7 minutes (set a timer) from the moment the last egg hits the water. Drain and pop the eggs into the bowl of iced water to cool off.

Leave for 10 minutes, then peel the eggs (it sometimes helps to peel under the water to keep them perfect) and drop into the soy mixture. Put a piece of paper towel over the eggs to keep them submerged, and place in the fridge. Leave overnight, then remove the eggs from the solution and transfer to an airtight container in the morning. They will keep for a week in the fridge (and the solution can be used for another round of eggs).

MUSHROOM MISO BROTH

Miso is a tired cook's best friend and the time-poor cook's shortcut to an excellent meal. In this instance, I've used brown rice miso, an earthy, boldly flavored miso, combining it with mushrooms for a delicious hot broth. It can be eaten on its own, but serving it with rice, as below, makes for a perfect lunch on an autumnal day.

Kombu is a flat natural seaweed which can be found dried in Asian supermarkets and health-food shops. It makes a great stock.

Serves 4 /

1⅔ cups jasmine rice

6 green onions

2 inches ginger, peeled and sliced

8 dried shiitake mushrooms

3 x 4-inch x 1-inch pieces kombu

1 bird's-eye chile, slit

½ lb mixed brown & shiitake mushrooms, finely sliced

¼ cup brown rice miso

First, cook the rice. Place the rice in a sieve and rinse under a cold tap until the water runs clear, then drain. Put the rice into a saucepan for which you have a lid, and cover with 2 cups of freshly boiled water. Bring to the boil, then place the lid on, turn the heat down, and simmer for 6 minutes. Turn the heat off but don't be tempted to lift the lid, and allow the rice to continue steaming until the soup is ready.

Next, make the soup. Pour 6½ cups of water into a large saucepan and set over a medium heat. Roughly chop 4 green onions and add to the pan with the ginger, dried shiitake, kombu, and chile. Bring to the boil, reduce the heat to low, and simmer for 10 minutes. Strain the stock through a fine sieve into a bowl, pouring it very carefully so you leave behind the last couple of tablespoons that might be a little gritty from the dried mushrooms. Return the broth to the pan and discard the stock vegetables.

Bring the broth back to the boil and, when gently bubbling, add the sliced mushrooms to the pan. Reduce the heat to a simmer and cook the mushrooms in the broth for 4 minutes. Remove the pan from the heat and add the miso. Whisk gently to incorporate, then divide the broth and mushrooms between four bowls. Finely slice the remaining 2 green onions, scatter over the broth, and serve alongside the steamed rice.

SWEET CHILE CASHEWS

V

Addictive, and the perfect sidekick to a G&T.

Serves a small crowd /

½ tsp salt

½ tsp red chile powder, such as Kashmiri

¼ tsp ground black pepper

3 tbsp sugar

2 cups unsalted cashews

First, line a baking sheet with parchment paper. Next, put the salt, chile powder, and black pepper into a small bowl, mix well, and leave to one side.

Put the sugar into a small frying pan over a medium heat and allow to melt into a clear pool without stirring. Once melted, tip in the cashews and spiced salt. Mix well, leave for a minute, and then mix again to glaze each of the nuts. Cook for another minute, until the sugar starts to cluster on the nuts, then tip onto the lined baking sheet. Press the nuts into a single layer with the back of a spoon and allow to cool completely.

Once cool, break any large clusters up with your hands (little clusters are fine and delicious, so feel free to leave those well alone) and place in a serving bowl.

salads

Salad often sits at the junction called "raw," just after "prepping," and just before "cooked," which is exactly why, for centuries, it was almost written out of India's culinary history. Given that water quality is still poor in many areas, raw vegetables are often associated with illness and so they haven't been used in the same way as they have been in other countries in South East Asia or the Western world. Even in big cities like Mumbai and Delhi, where signs in restaurants eagerly point out that their vegetables have been washed in "bottled water," salads are either in their infancy or take their lead from other countries. At worst, they are an afterthought by the chef: a few sliced onions and tomatoes on a plate.

Given my love of salad and Indian food, I have spent a lot of time in the middle of this Venn diagram, dreaming up what an Indian salad could look like. This chapter contains quite a few such imaginings.

Salads are a well-developed phenomenon in Thailand, Vietnam, and Burma, however, and are unbeatable for their sometimes clean, sometimes complex, but always invigorating flavors. My favorite Thai salads are the refreshing green papaya salad (som tam) and the lesser-known pomelo salad (yum som-o). Although both these salads use fruit, the fruit retains its sour bite and is perfectly balanced with a pounded dressing made using garlic, chile, sugar, and lime. Similar flavors are found in the famous Vietnamese dressing nuoc cham. Burmese salads, by contrast, have a much deeper savory base note to them, which comes from using roasted chickpea flour and crispy fried onions to dress the salad with. Piquancy in Burma is added using pickles: pickled ginger, pickled lemon, and even pickled fermented tea leaves.

Of course, salads are defined by different countries in different ways, but whatever the origin, what make a great salad, in my opinion, are the following three things.

Firstly, it must be clear what the salad's role is. I'm not talking about whether it is a side or a main, but whether the salad in question is balanced against the other dishes on the table so not everything is competing for your attention. For example, a brightly flavored salad might only need a simple rice dish alongside.

Secondly, it needs contrasting textures. This can be as simple as making sure you have crunchy vegetables alongside soft sweet herbs, or throwing in a handful of toasted nuts or crispy store-bought onions.

Thirdly, it needs shamelessly bold flavors. In East Asian salads this comes from the dressing, often an interplay between salt, sugar, acid, and heat. But it also comes from using large handfuls of herbs, a mixture of spices, or a pungent sauce like soy. As a rule of thumb, a dressing should always taste slightly stronger and saltier before you dress your salad than you'd like it to be ultimately, as it will become diluted in the salad.

Finally, a word to the wise. Salads are nearly always best when made or dressed just before serving. This is in part because leaves wilt, vegetables brown, and salted dressings draw out water from vegetables, making them soggy. No one loves wilted, brown sog, so keep it crisp and fresh and you won't go far wrong.

THAI SALAD with grapefruit and cashews   V

A great Thai salad hits you from different angles. One moment it's sweet, the next hot, crunchy then sour, and you feel it not only on your tongue but also in your head and stomach, and the heat even travels to the tips of your fingers. This salad is somewhere between the classic Thai som tam, and the lesser-known citrus salad yum som-o, made with pomelos. Be sure to dress it just before serving, as the longer it sits, the more juice the grapefruit will release and the less potent it will be.

Serves 4 as a side or 2 for lunch /

1 pink or red grapefruit

¼ cup lime juice

3 cups finely shredded red cabbage

½ lb carrots (2 medium), peeled and julienned

3 cups finely shredded iceberg lettuce

⅓ cup torn up Thai basil leaves

1 tsp salt

1 clove of garlic, crushed

2 bird's-eye chiles, very finely chopped

1½–2 tsp sugar (to taste)

1 tbsp soy sauce

2 tbsp canola oil

½ cup unsalted cashews, roughly chopped

⅔ cup crispy fried onions (store-bought)

Place the grapefruit on a chopping board and cut a third off the end. Squeeze the juice of this third into a small bowl to get around ¼ cup of juice. Add the lime juice and keep to one side.

Slice the peel off the other two-thirds of the grapefruit, cut the flesh into segments, and place in a large mixing bowl. Add the cabbage, carrots, lettuce, and all but a handful of the basil leaves and mix. Add the salt, mix again, and set aside while you make the dressing.

To make the dressing, pound the garlic, chiles, and sugar into a paste using a pestle and mortar. Add the soy sauce and muddle, then add the grapefruit and lime juice and mix again. If your pestle and mortar is large enough, add the oil and mix. If not, decant the dressing to a bowl, then add the oil and whisk to combine.

Pour the dressing over the salad, mix well, then tip onto a platter or into a salad bowl. Top with the remaining basil leaves, the chopped cashews, and the crispy fried onions, and serve immediately.

FORBIDDEN RICE SALAD with blistered broccolini and miso dressing

In the 1990s, black rice, once rare and "forbidden" to all but the Chinese aristocracy, was cross-pollinated with a type of Italian risotto rice to create a beautiful variety called venere nero. At around the same time, a Japanese seed scientist crossed Chinese kale with broccoli to produce a new vegetable whose stem is as delicious as its tip. It was named broccolini. This dish brings together these two plant-based creations—and it makes me wonder: what could we be eating in another few years' time?

note / Large supermarkets stock white miso and frozen podded edamame beans. They're also available online. You'll need a small blender to make the dressing. You can purchase venere nero rice online.

Serves 4 /

For the salad /

1½ cups venere nero rice

canola oil

½ lb broccolini

⅓ lb snow peas

1 avocado

3 cups shredded red cabbage

¾ cup thinly sliced radishes

1 cup frozen podded edamame beans, defrosted

For the dressing /

½ cup unsalted cashews

½ inch ginger, peeled and chopped

3½ tbsp white miso

2 tbsp canola oil

3½ tbsp lemon juice

1 tbsp agave syrup

1 tsp salt

Put the rice into a large pan, cover with plenty of water, and bring to the boil. Once boiling, turn down the heat to a simmer and cook for 18 minutes, until tender. Drain into a sieve, then set the sieve over the same pan, cover with a kitchen towel, and leave to one side.

Put all the dressing ingredients into a blender with ⅓ cup of water and whizz. Taste, and adjust the salt, lemon, and miso as you wish.

For the vegetables, heat 1½ tablespoons of canola oil in a large frying pan on a medium-high flame. Once hot, add the broccolini and cook for 2 minutes, then add a splash of water (about 3 tablespoons), toss, and cover with a lid. Leave to cook for 5 minutes, until tender, then transfer to a plate. Add another drizzle of oil to the pan and, when hot, add the snow peas. Cook for a couple of minutes until nicely blistered, then add to the plate with the broccolini.

To assemble the salad, put the cooked rice into a large serving bowl. Pit the avocado, then cut into wedges and peel. Layer the cabbage, broccolini, and snow peas over the rice, followed by the radishes, edamame, and avocado. Drizzle over the dressing, mix, and serve.

salads

TOMATO PONZU SALAD

V

Ponzu is a spiky, citrusy Japanese sauce which, in this recipe, is made using soy, lemon, and tangerine juice. When combined with the best tomatoes you can get your hands on, the citrus and salt take flight and elevate this into something very special.

Serves 4 as a side /

For the ponzu sauce /

1 tbsp toasted sesame oil

3 tbsp tangerine juice
   (from 1 tangerine)

1 tbsp lemon juice

2 tbsp soy sauce, or to taste

For the tomatoes /

1 lb ripe sweet cherry tomatoes,
   quartered

1 large or 2 small shallots,
   thinly sliced

a handful of fresh Thai basil
   or tarragon leaves

Place all the ingredients for the ponzu sauce in a small bowl and mix. Taste to check you're happy with the seasoning: as citrus fruits vary, you may need to add more tangerine juice for sweetness, more lemon juice for sharpness, or more soy sauce to balance it.

Place the tomatoes and shallots in a serving bowl and pour the ponzu over the top. If the leaves of the herbs are quite big, rip them; if not, place them whole in the salad. Leave at room temperature for an hour or so for the flavors to mingle, then serve.

CHARGRILLED SUMMER VEGETABLES V
with a dhana-jeera dressing

Salads have not always been common fare in India due to poor water quality, but times are changing now and salads are gaining a place at the table. However, there's a lot of ground to make up, and I often wonder what future Indian salads might look like. This salad is such an imagining, using some of summer's finest produce alongside India's most notorious spice duo: cumin and coriander, or dhana jeera. Used with abandon in everyday curries, here they get a fresh lease on life, and the result is smoky, sweet, crisp, and lip-tingling.

note / You can cook this salad on an outdoor grill or grill pan indoors. The timings are for a grill pan, so if you're grilling outdoors, cook the vegetables until tender.

Serves 4 /

canola oil

¾ tsp salt

1¼ tsp ground cumin

1½ tsp ground coriander

¾ tsp red chile powder, such as Kashmiri

2 tbsp lemon juice

2 zucchini

⅔ lb broccolini

2 medium red onions

2 corn cobs, dehusked

First, make the dressing. Put ¼ cup of oil into a small bowl, add the salt, cumin, coriander, chile powder, and lemon juice, and set aside.

Cut the zucchini lengthways into ¼-inch-thick slices. Trim the broccolini, and break bigger branches into individual stems. Peel and cut the onions into eighths. (If grilling, separate the onions into "petals.") Put a grill pan on a high flame. Brush the vegetables all over with oil, and dunk the broccolini in oil, so the florets are coated. When the pan is very hot, lay in the zucchini in a single layer and grill for 2 minutes on each side, until pleasingly striped, then transfer to a platter.

Grill the onions for 5 minutes, until soft and blackened, then place on top of the zucchini. Grill the broccolini for 1½ to 3 minutes: you want to cook the stems without burning the florets, so use tongs to press the stems down, adding a splash of water to create some steam. Once tender, place on top of the onions.

Using tongs, hold each cob over a medium flame on the stovetop for about 5 minutes, rotating every 30 seconds or so, when the kernels start to blister and char. When the corn is cool enough to handle, stand it up in a bowl and cut down the length of the cob, close to the core, to shuck the kernels. Scatter these on top of the salad, whisk the dressing with a fork, pour over the top, and gently toss to coat. Serve warm or at room temperature.

PANEER, SPINACH, AND TOMATO SALAD

Saag paneer, given a fresh new makeover.

Serves 4 as a main /

2 lbs ripe tomatoes, large ones halved or quartered

5 cloves of garlic, unpeeled

¼ cup canola oil, divided

2 tsp salt

2 medium red onions

8 oz paneer, cut into ¾-inch cubes

1 tsp ground cumin

1 tsp red chile powder, such as Kashmiri

1 tsp garam masala

1 tbsp lemon juice

1 naan bread, cut into wedges

4 packed cups baby-leaf spinach

Preheat the oven to 425°F.

Place the tomatoes in a roasting pan along with the garlic, then drizzle with 1 tablespoon of oil and ½ teaspoon of salt. Peel the onions, cut into ¾-inch wedges and put them into a separate roasting pan with the paneer, shuffling them into a single layer. Drizzle with 1 tablespoon of oil and sprinkle over another ½ teaspoon of salt. Place both pans in the oven for 25 minutes.

While the pans are in the oven, make the dressing. Combine the cumin, chile powder, garam masala, lemon juice, 2 tablespoons of oil, and 1 teaspoon of salt and whisk together.

When the 25 minutes are up, remove the onion pan from the oven, add the naan, and toss together so the naan becomes coated in the oniony oil. Return to the oven and cook both pans for a further 8 minutes until the bread is crisp and brown at the edges, the onions are soft and burnished, and the tomatoes have blackened spots on them.

Use a slotted spoon to fish out the cloves of garlic and, when cool enough to handle, squeeze the soft flesh into the dressing and mix. Add the tomatoes to the onions, paneer, and naan, leaving some of the juices behind. Add the spinach and dressing, and enough of the tomato juices so that everything is coated and well mixed. Taste, adjust the seasoning if you like, and serve.

CHARRED ROMAINE LETTUCE
with mint raita

Once you've chargrilled a lettuce and found bliss in its bitter blackened edges and soft, sweet heart, it's hard to go back. The dressing here is based on a classic mint raita, but without the sugar—which makes it hotter and more tangy, in a very good way. You can char the lettuce on a grill pan or briefly over indirect heat on the grill.

note / You'll need a blender for this recipe.

Serves 4 as a side /

¾ cup mint leaves

½ a green finger (or serrano) chile,
   finely chopped

¼ tsp ground cumin

½ tbsp lime juice
   (from ½ a lime)

¾ cup Greek yogurt (non-dairy
   if vegan)

salt

1 tbsp canola oil

2 romaine lettuce hearts, halved
   lengthways

Start by making the raita. In a blender, combine the mint leaves, chile, cumin, lime juice, yogurt, and ¼ teaspoon of salt. Blitz until smooth, empty into a small bowl, and leave to one side while you char the lettuce.

Heat a grill pan over a high flame. Combine the oil and ½ teaspoon of salt in a bowl, then brush over the cut sides of the lettuce. Place the lettuce halves face down on the pan and cook for 4 minutes on the first side, or until charred, with the outer leaves crisping at the edges. Turn and cook for a further 2 minutes. The lettuce should still hold its shape.

Arrange the lettuce on a platter and drizzle with as much raita as you wish. Serve the rest in a bowl on the table.

BURMESE MANGO SALAD
with peanut and lime

V

This is inspired by a dish I ate at one of my favorite restaurants in Mumbai, called Burma Burma. So it is that I offer up my memory of its mighty and mouthwatering mango, peanut, and lime salad.

note / When freshly made, this salad is great by itself or with seasoned and fried tofu, but if left a day it will release delicious juices and is wonderful with rice noodles. You can hand-cut the long strips of mango and carrot, but a julienne peeler will make quick work of it. Make sure you buy the hardest, greenest, most unripe mangoes you can find, because ripe mangoes will juice when you cut them.

Serves 4 /

¾ inch fresh ginger, peeled and julienned

1 bird's-eye chile, finely chopped

¼ cup + 1 tbsp lime juice

1 tsp salt

canola oil

1 medium onion, halved and thinly sliced

4 cloves of garlic, thinly sliced

1½ tbsp chickpea flour

2 tbsp crunchy peanut butter

3 cups finely shredded napa cabbage

1 lb unripe mangoes (approx 1 mango)

½ lb carrots (2 medium), peeled and julienned

a handful of fresh mint leaves

a handful of fresh cilantro leaves

½ cup salted peanuts, crushed

Put the ginger and chile into a bowl, add the lime juice and salt, and leave to steep.

Put a plate by the stove and cover it with a piece of kitchen paper. Heat 5 tablespoons of oil in a non-stick frying pan over a medium flame and, when smoking hot, add the onion. Separate the slices using a wooden spoon and fry, stirring once or twice, until brown and crisp. Scoop out with a slotted spoon and put on the prepared plate. Fry the garlic in the same pan for 2 minutes, until golden brown (be watchful: it cooks quickly), then transfer to the plate.

Stir the chickpea flour into the remaining hot oil in the pan over a very low heat to create a paste. Stir constantly for a minute, then add the peanut butter, stir for another minute, and take off the heat.

Put the cabbage into a large bowl. Peel the mangoes and shave with a julienne peeler until you hit the pit; or, if cutting by hand, cut the cheeks from the pit on all four sides and julienne. Add the mango and carrots to the cabbage. Reserve a handful of the fried onion to garnish, then add the rest, together with the fried garlic, to the cabbage. Toss, then pour over the chickpea and peanut paste and the ginger, chile, and lime mixture, and toss again. Taste, and adjust the lime and salt if need be. To serve, finely chop and add the herbs, toss one final time, and top with the crushed peanuts and remaining fried onion.

See photo overleaf

BURMESE MANGO SALAD WITH PEANUT AND LIME

ASPARAGUS AND SNOW PEAS
with chile peanut crumbs

When it comes to cooking certain vegetables such as asparagus, less is more. But there is a time and a place to break the rules.

note / If you're using regular asparagus, just halve it lengthways.

Serves 4 as a side /

⅓ cup unsalted peanuts

¼ cup canola oil, divided

2 cloves of garlic, finely sliced

1 bird's-eye chile, finely sliced

¾ cup breadcrumbs

½ tsp salt

1½ tbsp lemon juice

¾ lb fine asparagus, bottoms
   trimmed

½ lb snow peas

First, bash the peanuts using a pestle and mortar until fairly well ground.

Next, take a large frying pan for which you have a lid and place over a medium-high heat. Warm 2 tablespoons of oil and, when hot, add the garlic. Fry for 1 minute, until just starting to brown, then add the chile and peanuts. Fry for a further minute, then stir in the breadcrumbs and salt, and fry for a further 2 minutes, stirring regularly, until the breadcrumbs are darkening and the peanuts are showing touches of brown. Add the lemon juice, stir to combine, and empty it all into a bowl.

Carefully wipe the pan clean with a paper towel and return to the stove. Heat a tablespoon of oil in the pan and add the asparagus, shaking the pan gently so the asparagus falls into a single layer. Cook for 2 minutes, giving the pan a little shake halfway through. Put the lid on and steam for a final minute, then tip the asparagus onto a platter.

Heat the final tablespoon of oil and add the snow peas, cook for 2 minutes, then return the asparagus to the pan. Toss all the veg together with half the peanut chile crumbs, then transfer to a serving platter and finish with the remainder of the crumbs.

salads

AVOCADO KACHUMBAR
VO

A tale of two salads (or a salad of two halves): silky-smooth thick cream made of avocado and yogurt, topped with crunchy fresh vegetables marinated in a lemon and oil dressing. This is great alongside slices of hot naan bread and can be used as a side, or as a dip to serve a crowd.

note / You'll need a blender for this recipe.

Serves 4 as a side /

½ a cucumber

10 radishes, trimmed and quartered

¼ of a medium red onion, very finely chopped

3 medium ripe tomatoes, cut into ½ in dice

5 sprigs of fresh mint, leaves picked and chopped

3 tbsp canola oil

zest and juice of 1 lemon

salt

3 avocados

½ cup Greek yogurt, or thick non-dairy yogurt, if vegan

Cut the cucumber in half lengthways and run a teaspoon down the middle to scrape out the seeds. Discard, then chop the flesh into ½-inch cubes. Place in a bowl with the radishes, red onion, tomatoes, mint, oil, lemon zest, and 1 tablespoon of lemon juice. Season with ⅓ teaspoon of salt, and taste and adjust as you see fit.

Make the avocado dip just before serving. Pit the avocados and place the flesh (you should get around 1 cup) in a blender with the yogurt, remaining tablespoon of lemon juice and ⅓ teaspoon of salt. Taste, and adjust if need be.

To serve, pour the avocado dip onto a lipped serving plate, and use the back of a spoon to smooth it out to the edges of the plate. Using a slotted spoon, pile the chopped vegetables into the center, and finish with a drizzle of the vegetable juices.

DOUBLE RAINBOW SALAD

This salad is so called due to the magic moment of alchemy I experienced when a few vegetables came together in perfect harmony, much like when the sun's light refracts through the water droplets in the atmosphere to form a rainbow. Well, that and it is a very pretty and colorful salad (in both looks and personality) to serve to guests.

note / Substitute radishes for the kohlrabi and daikon if you can't find them. You'll need a blender for this recipe.

Serves 4 as a side /

4 cups finely sliced red cabbage

1 medium carrot, peeled and cut into thin coins

1 cup frozen podded edamame beans, defrosted

2 cups matchsticks of kohlrabi or daikon

3 packed cups baby-leaf spinach

¼ cup + 1 tbsp toasted sesame oil

2 tbsp canola oil

1 cup roughly chopped cilantro leaves

2 tbsp lime juice (from 1½ limes)

½ inch ginger, peeled and roughly chopped

1 clove of garlic, roughly chopped

1 tsp salt

1 tsp chile flakes

Put the cabbage, carrot, edamame, kohlrabi, and spinach into a large serving bowl.

To make the dressing, put the oils, cilantro, lime juice, ginger, garlic, salt, and chile flakes into a blender and whizz until smooth. Scrape out every last bit into the salad bowl and mix using your hands—which will help wilt the salad a little—just before serving.

CARAMELIZED FENNEL AND CARROT SALAD with mung beans and herbs

V

The long-neglected mung bean has much to give if you let it into your kitchen. Cooked quickly, it becomes a nutty addition to a salad; cooked slowly, and you'll find yourself with a creamy dal; soak it, and it will magically sprout, like Jack's beanstalk.

Serves 4 /

1 lb carrots (2 large), peeled and cut into thin batons

1 lb fennel bulbs (2 medium), thinly sliced, fronds reserved

3 cloves of garlic, unpeeled

olive oil

salt

1 tsp chile flakes

¾ cup mung beans

¾ cup giant (Israeli) couscous

For the dressing /

¾ cup Italian parsley leaves

¾ cup mint leaves

¾ cup dill leaves

1½ tbsp lemon juice

1 tbsp capers, drained and chopped

1 tsp Dijon mustard

Preheat the oven to 425°F and line two baking sheets with foil.

Lay the carrots, fennel, and garlic in a single layer across the two sheets. Mix ¼ cup of oil, ½ teaspoon of salt, and the chile flakes in a small bowl, spoon over the vegetables, then toss with your hands to make sure everything is well coated. Roast for 30 minutes, or until tender and beginning to char, tossing the vegetables halfway through to ensure they cook evenly.

In the meantime, put the mung beans into a saucepan, cover with plenty of cold water, bring to the boil, then simmer for 15 minutes. Add the couscous to the pan, turn up the heat, and boil for 6 to 8 minutes until tender, then drain thoroughly.

To make the dressing, finely chop the herb leaves with the fennel fronds, then put into a bowl and add the chopped flesh of the roasted garlic, the lemon juice, capers, mustard, and ¼ teaspoon of salt. Add enough olive oil to make a dressing (roughly 3 to 5 tablespoons), mix very well, then taste and adjust as you see fit.

To assemble the salad, spoon the warm mung beans and couscous onto a serving plate, lay the vegetables on top, then mix in the green herb dressing to taste and serve.

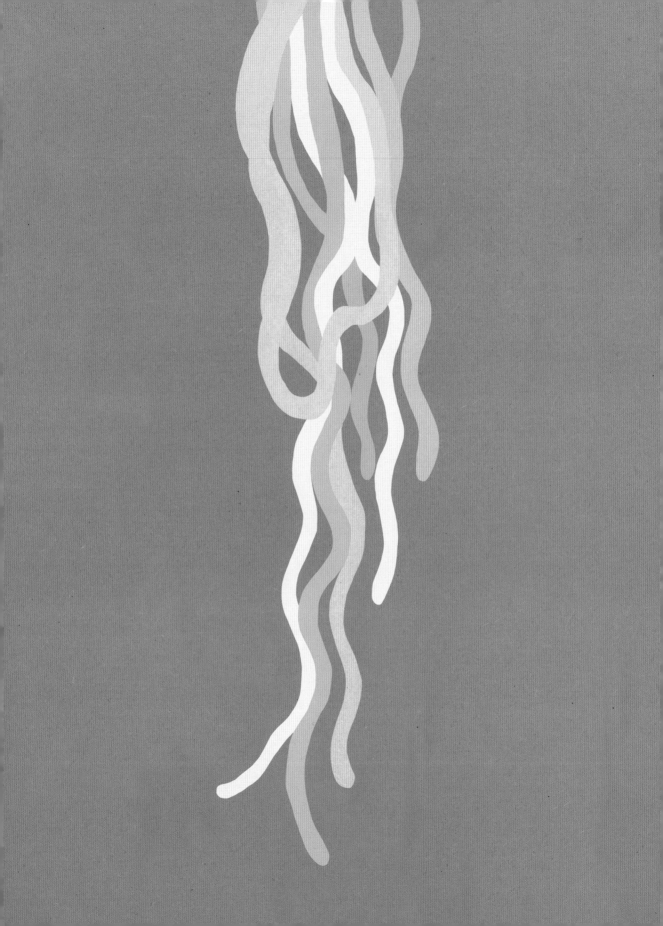

noodles

Say the word and you form the shape with your mouth.

For years, the only noodle I knew was Sharwood's Medium Egg. As reliable as a Labrador, they were cooked in our house in the way that is common in Indian houses: in an Indian-Chinese-style stir-fry with lots of chile, garlic, ketchup, soy sauce, and whichever vegetables happened to be at hand. After many years and multiple trips to Chinatowns up and down the country, I learned to move beyond "Medium Egg" and unravel the vexed subject of the noodle, so here's a quick guide to choosing, cooking, and handling all the different varieties.

COOKING AND PORTION SIZE

The first step to mastering noodles is preparation. For many noodle dishes you need to throw the ingredients into the pan in quick succession before the noodles are mixed in, so make sure you have all your ingredients chopped and ready to go. In many cases, this means having the noodles cooked and ready too (which I'll come to next).

To boil or to soak?

Most wheat-based noodles can be boiled in plenty of water, just like pasta. You can follow the timings on the package, but again, just as with pasta, when the insides are no longer crunchy or chalky, the noodles are cooked. Rice noodles are a little different in that most cooking instructions call for soaking in freshly boiled water, with no active "cooking." Whichever way you cook your noodles, if you're using them in a stir-fried dish, it's a good idea to take them out of the water just shy of being "done," because you'll be reheating and cooking them again in the pan.

Drain and refresh

Where a recipe asks you to have your noodles prepared in advance, it's best to stop them from cooking and clumping by placing them in a colander, rinsing them with plenty of cold water, allowing them to drain, and rubbing through a little oil, using your hands.

Mixing

Mixing pre-cooked noodles into vegetables or a sauce is an art. Ensure you have a big enough pan or bowl and a good tool, like a spaghetti fork or a pair of salad servers, to help. Metal utensils can cut noodles and wooden spoons are no good to you here.

Portion size

Most packages suggest 2–3 oz of noodles per person. Personally, I find 3–4 oz more appropriate for a dry noodle dish and around 1½–2½ oz perfect for noodle soup, but as with all portion sizes it depends on what else is going into the dish, the type of noodle, and, of course, people's appetites.

TYPES OF NOODLES

Wheat noodles

Whole wheat noodles

These are the workhorse of my noodle cupboard. I like them for their square shape, delicious wholemeal flavor, and versatility (you can use them in both stir-fries and soups). They're widely available, suitable for vegans, and easy to work with.

Egg noodles

These nests, curled up like the peaks of Hokusai's *Great Wave*, are most commonly associated with dishes like Chinese chow mein and generally cook within just 4 minutes. Although they are called "egg noodles" they are predominantly made from wheat and can contain anywhere from 5 to 15 percent egg. The egg, in my experience, gives the noodle a fraction more bounce, richness, and slipperiness than the slightly stickier whole wheat noodle, but you can use either in the recipes in this chapter.

Ramen noodles

Ramen noodles are made from wheat with the special addition of alkaline salts, which ensures they don't turn to mush in a hot soupy ramen. How "al dente" the ramen noodle should be when served appears to be a hotly debated subject in Japan: in some ramen restaurants you can ask for your noodles to be *yowarakame*, meaning "soft," *futsuu*, "normal," or even *katamen*, "hard." I am quite a slow eater and therefore enjoy mine hard. Play around with the cooking times: don't be afraid to undercook them and see if you prefer them that way. Available dried in big supermarkets, Asian grocery stores, and online.

Udon noodles

These are my secret favorite for their big bounce and table-silencing chewiness. They are made from wheat and water and are available both dried and partially cooked. Dried udon noodles are similar to fat fettuccine, but the partially cooked "straight to wok" or frozen udon noodles are as thick as a pencil and nice and plump. Both are available from supermarkets and Asian grocery stores.

GLASS NOODLES

RAMEN NOODLES

BUCKWHEAT SOBA

RICE STICKS

EGG NOODLES

UDON

RICE VERMICELLI

WHOLE
WHEAT

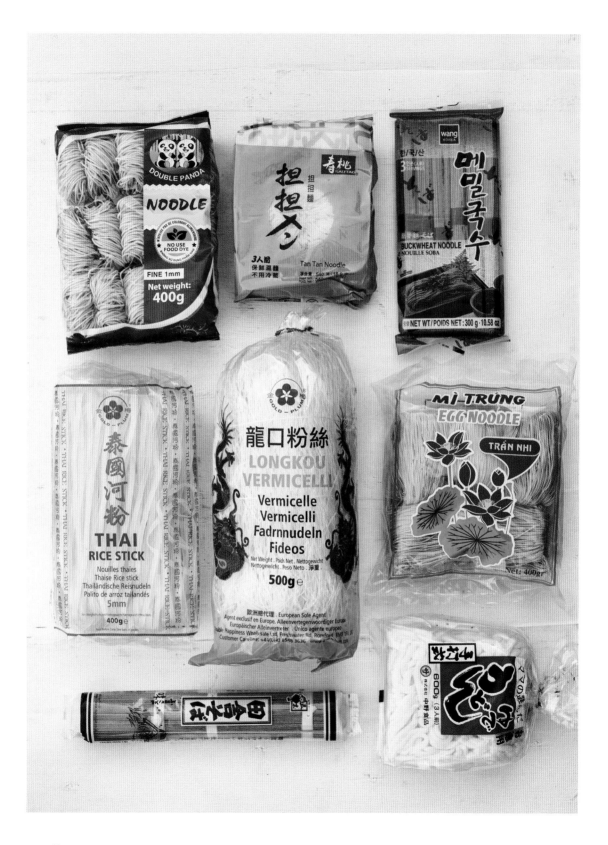

noodles

Buckwheat soba noodles

These Japanese noodles are made from anything between 10 and 100 percent buckwheat flour (the rest being wheat). They have a very slippery texture and a smashing nutty flavor. Traditionally, they are served cold with a dipping sauce or hot in a broth. In the summer I love to eat these noodles cold, coated in a sauce made with herbs and pistachios (see page 91). They're available dried in supermarkets and Asian grocery stores.

Rice noodles

Rice vermicelli noodles

Vermicelli noodles are playful. Having a hundred little wriggly noodles attached to my chopsticks or mouth is my idea of a good time at the table. They're most famously used in Singapore noodles (see page 95) but also in bun cha, the fresh and zingy Vietnamese salad (see page 181). They are gluten-free, which is great for people with celiac disease, and they are available in most supermarkets.

Rice sticks

These thin rice noodles, around ¼-inch wide, are used for pad thai and are very similar to the noodles which are used in Vietnamese soup, pho. They're found in Asian grocery stores, but you'll find folded "medium rice" noodles in most supermarkets and these make a good substitute.

Other noodles

Glass noodles

Glass noodles go under various names and are often called cellophane noodles or bean thread noodles. They look much like rice vermicelli noodles, but as their name suggests they're glass-like in appearance. They're most commonly made using mung bean starch (which are the ones I use in the Thai clay pot noodles on page 84), but they can also be made from sweet potato starch or pea starch. They are wonderfully slippery and absorb flavors very well. You may need to cut them with scissors as they can be quite long (too long to fit into most of my saucepans). Available from Asian grocery stores or online, the best way to cook them is to soak them in boiling water until tender.

noodles

BREAKFAST AT SHUKO'S

When Shuko Oda first opened Koya in Soho, Central London, rumors spread around the city like hot butter. Firstly, Shuko had created some of the finest udon noodles anyone could eat without jumping on a plane to Japan. Secondly, these noodles were kneaded by foot! It transpired that both of these rumors were true, and suddenly everyone flocked to worship at the altar of this modestly brilliant place.

This dish, kama tama (or raw egg and soy udon noodles), is on the breakfast menu at Koya, although in my opinion it makes for a lovely quick lunch too. The recipe might only have three key ingredients, but it is as sophisticated as it is simple to make.

note / The best udon noodles to use here are the plump, partially cooked "straight to wok" noodles. If you use dried noodles, you'll only need 7 oz and a tablespoon of additional water to loosen when you mix them with the egg yolks and soy.

Serves 2 /

1½ x 7-oz packages straight to wok
   udon noodles
2 large egg yolks
1 tbsp soy sauce
optional: 1 sheet of nori, shredded

Bring a large pan of water to a rolling boil, then drop in the noodles and cook until they are al dente. This should take around 3 minutes for the "straight to wok" udons or 4 to 7 minutes if you're using the dried type.

Meanwhile, in a large mixing bowl, mix together the egg yolks and soy sauce. When the noodles are cooked, drain well and immediately add to the egg mixture, mixing really well so they are coated in the sauce. Divide the noodles between two bowls, and sprinkle with shredded nori if you like. Serve immediately.

RUTABAGA LAKSA

A wise man (OK, restaurant critic Jay Rayner) once said of laksa's medicinal properties that "it should be available on the NHS (the National Health Service) by prescription," and I agree. With its searing chile, ginger, and garlic enveloped by a blanket of noodles and coconut soup, laksa is a wonderful antidote to colds and cold weather. I urge any rutabaga dodgers to think twice: its buttery earthiness, alongside the caramelized shallots, adds a sweet and smoky magic.

Serves 4 /

6 cloves of garlic, roughly chopped

1 inch ginger, peeled and roughly chopped

4 tsp red chile powder, such as Kashmiri

2½ tsp ground cumin

2 lemongrass stalks, bottom 2 inches only, roughly chopped

¾ cup packed cilantro, stems and leaves divided

4¼ cups vegan vegetable stock

6 shallots

canola oil

1 x 14-oz can of coconut milk

1½ tsp salt

1½ tsp sugar

2 lbs rutabaga (¾ of a large one), peeled

7 oz rice vermicelli noodles

2 limes, cut into wedges

Preheat the oven to 425°F and line two large baking sheets with foil.

To make the laksa paste, put the garlic, ginger, chile powder, cumin, lemongrass, and cilantro stems into a blender with ⅔ cup of stock. Peel and roughly chop 2 shallots and add them to the blender too, then whizz to a paste.

Heat 2 tablespoons of oil in a deep-sided pot on a low flame and, once hot, scrape the paste into the pot. Cook for 10 to 15 minutes, stirring regularly so it doesn't catch, then slowly add the coconut milk until it's mixed in. Add the remaining stock, the salt, and sugar, and simmer for 20 minutes until rich and flavorful. Season to taste, then take off the heat.

While the soup is cooking, halve the rutabaga, cut it into ½-inch-thick slices, then arrange on one of the lined sheets. Peel and halve the remaining shallots lengthways, then separate them into "petals" by removing the individual segments, and put these on the second lined sheet. Lightly drizzle oil over both vegetables, toss with your hands so they're well coated, and sprinkle with a little salt. Roast the shallots for 20 minutes and the rutabaga for 30 minutes, until cooked and caramelized.

Cook the noodles in boiling water as per the package instructions (usually 2 to 3 minutes), then drain and rinse under cold water.

To serve, reheat the soup on a medium heat. Distribute the noodles between four bowls and ladle over the hot soup. Put the hot rutabaga and caramelized shallots on top and sprinkle with cilantro leaves. Squeeze a wedge of lime over each serving, and serve with more lime on the side.

BEN BEN NOODLES

V

It burst my bubble when I found out that dan dan noodles, the infamous Sichuanese dish, was not named after two men called Dan but the type of pole used by street-sellers to carry baskets of noodles and sauce. But in this instance, the name "ben ben" refers to my friend, the great cook Ben Benton, on whose recipe this dish is based. Here, shiitake mushrooms rub alongside tahini and chile oil to make an astoundingly good sauce that is hot enough to put hairs on your chest.

note / You might need to hop into an Asian supermarket for the Chinkiang vinegar and chile oil—but if that's not an option you could substitute balsamic or white wine vinegar for the Chinkiang, and make your own chile oil (see page 257). You'll need a food processor for the mushrooms.

Serves 2, generously /

½ lb fresh shiitake mushrooms

1 tsp Sichuan peppercorns

1 tbsp canola oil

2½ tbsp finely chopped sweet and sour pickles

2 green onions, sliced diagonally

1 tbsp Shaoxing rice wine

2 tsp soy sauce

7 oz whole wheat noodles

7 oz choy sum or baby bok choy, quartered

For the sauce /

3 tbsp tahini

3 tbsp soy sauce

1 tbsp chile oil, with sediment to taste

1 tbsp Chinkiang vinegar

Place the mushrooms in a food processor and blitz to lentil-sized pieces (but be careful they don't turn to soup). Put the peppercorns in a dry frying pan over a low flame and toast for around 4 minutes until fragrant, then grind with a pestle and mortar and set aside.

In the same pan, heat the oil over a high flame. Add the mushrooms and fry for 8 to 10 minutes until dark brown and beginning to crisp, pressing into a single layer with the back of a spoon to maximize crisping potential. Add the pickles, the green onions, and the ground Sichuan pepper, and fry for 2 minutes. Add the rice wine and soy sauce, and continue to cook for a further 2 minutes until dry and crunchy.

To make the sauce, mix all the ingredients together in a small bowl. The sauce will look a little split at first, but just keep mixing until it comes together. Cook the noodles according to the package instructions, stirring to separate the noodles and adding the greens for the final 2 minutes.

Just before the noodles have finished cooking, fill a mug with the noodle cooking water. Drain the noodles and greens, place the greens to one side and the noodles in a bowl. Mix the sauce into the noodles and add the cooking water, tablespoon by tablespoon (I needed 6) until the noodles are nice and saucy.

Divide between two plates and put the mushroom mixture on top and the greens to the side of each bowl.

PEANUT BUTTER AND BROCCOLINI PAD THAI

In the late 1930s, Thailand's prime minister held a public competition to find a new national dish. The winning entry combined rice noodles, vegetables, peanuts, shrimp, and egg. It was named "pad thai" (*pad* meaning "stir-fry") in a bid to promote a sense of Thai-ness. This vegan interpretation of that classic dish celebrates the brilliance of the original, while also bringing something new in the form of broccolini.

note / Pad thai is best eaten with as many garnishes as possible, so feel free to customize yours with fried shallots, pickled vegetables, and crushed peanuts as you wish. Rice noodles are fragile, so be gentle with them.

Serves 4 /

For the pad thai sauce /

⅓ cup crunchy peanut butter

2 tbsp tamarind paste

3 tbsp agave syrup

¼ cup soy sauce

3 tbsp fresh lime juice (from approx. 2 limes)

For the tofu and broccolini /

1 lb broccolini

3 cloves of garlic, crushed

½ inch ginger, peeled and grated

2 bird's-eye chiles, finely chopped

8 oz firm tofu, drained and cubed

9 oz flat folded rice noodles

canola oil

6 green onions, finely chopped

a handful of sesame seeds

toasted sesame oil

a handful of fresh Thai basil leaves, shredded

a handful of fresh mint leaves, shredded

1 lime, cut into 4 wedges

First, make the sauce by putting the peanut butter, tamarind paste, and agave syrup into a bowl, then slowly mixing in the soy sauce, lime juice, and ¼ cup of water.

Next, trim the broccolini, and put the florets into a bowl. Chop the stalks and leaves into ½-inch pieces. Place the garlic, ginger, chiles, and tofu in little piles within easy reach of the stovetop. Cook the noodles according to the package instructions, rinse under cold water, drain, then drizzle with a tablespoon of canola oil and toss gently with your hands.

In a large non-stick frying pan for which you have a lid, heat 2 tablespoons of canola oil on a medium-high flame, then fry the tofu for 5 minutes, turning every minute, until it's pale gold. Add the garlic, ginger, and chiles, cook for 2 minutes, then add the broccolini stalks and ¼ cup of water, cover the pan, and steam for 2 minutes, until the broccolini is tender. Add the broccolini florets, sauce, and green onions (reserve a handful for garnish), stir to combine, then cover again and leave for 2 minutes.

Turn the heat down to a whisper, add the noodles handful by handful, gently mixing them in until coated in sauce, then turn off the heat. Distribute the noodles between four plates and sprinkle over the sesame seeds and reserved green onions. Drizzle each portion with sesame oil, scatter over the herbs, add a generous squeeze of lime, and serve immediately.

noodles

MOUTH-NUMBING NOODLES with chile oil and red cabbage

V

We need to talk about heat—not just the kind that comes from fresh chiles, but from peppercorns, ginger, horseradish, or too much garlic. Heat can be many things but our language holds us back and so these ingredients are usually described in a one-size-fits-all way, as simply "mild," "medium," or "hot."

The hero of this dish, the Sichuan peppercorn, is a case in point. Muddy pink in color, smelling of grapefruit, the Sichuan pepper lends an unusual citrus flavor to whatever it touches, creating a unique lip-tingling and mouth-numbing sensation—which isn't at all "hot."

note / You'll need a blender or electric spice grinder. Any leftover chile oil can be kept in the fridge for a couple of weeks.

Serves 4 /

For the pickled cabbage /

3 cups finely shredded red cabbage

½ a cucumber, seeds scraped out, sliced thinly

a handful of fresh mint leaves, chopped

¼ cup rice vinegar

1 tbsp toasted sesame oil

salt

1 tbsp sesame seeds

For the mouth-numbing chile oil /

2 tbsp Sichuan peppercorns

¼ cup chile flakes

⅓ cup canola oil

4 cloves of garlic, finely chopped

1 tsp sugar

For the noodles /

¼ cup crunchy peanut butter

¼ cup toasted sesame oil

14 oz whole wheat noodles

To make the pickled cabbage, put the cabbage, cucumber, and mint into a bowl, add the vinegar, sesame oil, and a pinch of salt, and mix with your hands. Scatter with the sesame seeds and leave to one side.

In a blender or spice grinder, blitz the peppercorns and chile flakes to a rough powder. Heat the canola oil in a small saucepan over a medium flame, then add the garlic and let it sizzle for a minute or two, until it turns a pale gold. Stir in the sugar, ½ teaspoon of salt, and the ground peppercorn and chile mixture, and take off the heat.

For the noodles, mix the peanut butter and sesame oil in a bowl with ⅓ teaspoon of salt. Cook the noodles according to the package instructions, then drain, rinse under cold water, and drain again. Put the noodles into a bowl, and add the peanut mixture and 2 tablespoons of chile oil. Toss with your hands, making sure all the noodles are well coated, then season to taste.

To serve, lift the noodles on to a platter (or into four shallow bowls), top with the sharp crunchy cabbage, then add a drizzle of chile oil, depending on your threshold for mouth-numbing heat.

noodles

WHITE MISO RAMEN with tofu and asparagus

V

In an unassuming corner of Westfield in Stratford, east London, is a joyful little Japanese canteen called Shoryu, where I had my mind blown by a ramen dish called "white natural." Unlike pork-dominated ramen dishes, white natural is made with soy milk and white miso, making it intensely silky. With apologies to Shoryu, I have tried to replicate it here.

note / You'll need a blender to make this. Don't be put off by the ingredients list: most of it goes straight into the blender. A good quality brand of soy milk, like Silk, is best for this recipe.

Serves 4 /

For the noodle soup /

¼ cup dried shiitake mushrooms

1 onion, chopped

4 cloves of garlic, roughly chopped

¾ inch ginger, peeled and roughly chopped

⅓ cup white miso

1 tbsp tahini

2 tbsp canola oil

3 tbsp soy sauce

1 quart soy milk

salt

9 oz ramen noodles

For the tofu and asparagus /

canola oil

½ lb fine asparagus (or normal asparagus halved lengthwise)

⅔ cup frozen podded edamame beans, defrosted

2 cloves of garlic, finely sliced

½ tsp chile flakes

⅓ tsp salt

½ tbsp lemon juice

10 oz extra-firm tofu, drained and cut into 1-inch cubes

1 tbsp soy sauce

First, make the noodle soup. Put the dried shiitake into a heatproof bowl, cover with ¾ cup of just-boiled water, and leave to soak for 5 minutes. In a blender, blitz the mushrooms (with their soaking liquid), onion, garlic, ginger, miso, tahini, oil, and soy sauce. Put a non-stick frying pan on a medium heat and, when hot, scrape the paste out of the blender and into the pan. Cook for 10 minutes, stirring frequently, then add the soy milk, little by little, until it's all mixed in—make sure it doesn't boil, or it may curdle—then add salt, if need be, and take off the heat.

Next, cook the noodles according to the package instructions, drain, rinse under cold water, and drain again.

Heat a tablespoon of oil in a large frying pan over a high flame. When it's smoking hot, throw in the asparagus and edamame, leave for a minute, then turn and leave for a minute more, so both char a little. Add the garlic, chile, salt, and lemon juice to the pan, stir for a minute, then transfer to a bowl.

In the same pan, heat another tablespoon of oil if needed, then fry the tofu for a minute on each side, until golden and crisp (when it's ready, you'll be able to turn the cubes easily with a spatula). Add the soy sauce to the tofu and gently mix, then transfer to the asparagus bowl.

To assemble, divide the noodles between four bowls. Reheat the miso soup if you need to, and share among the bowls. Lay some tofu cubes on one side of each bowl, share out the asparagus and edamame evenly, and serve hot.

CLAY POT NOODLES with beets and smoked tofu

I've been to Bangkok a few times but never met clay pot noodles. My first encounter was in Soho, London, at a restaurant called Kiln. From the start, my mouth did not know what had hit it. It was as mind-altering as watching Disney's *Fantasia* as a seven-year-old. In my recipe, I've used smoked tofu slices, beets, and walnuts to create some rich, almost meaty flavors and, as a bonus, the noodles turn pink. This is a special occasion or weekend dish as it requires a little more effort.

note / Smoked tofu and kecap manis can be found in bigger supermarkets or online; to make your own kecap manis, see page 256. The noodles you need here are glass noodles made from 100 percent mung bean starch—they can be found in Asian supermarkets or online. If you don't have a clay pot, a 10-inch casserole dish will do. You'll also need a food processor for this recipe.

Serves 4 /

7 oz mung bean glass noodles

1 tbsp soy sauce

½ a medium red onion, chopped

½ inch ginger, peeled

5 cloves of garlic, chopped

1 lb raw beets, peeled and roughly chopped

¾ cup walnuts, plus 2 tbsp to garnish

½ cup packed chopped cilantro, leaves and stems divided

¼ cup canola oil

1 tsp salt

⅔ tsp ground black pepper

7 oz smoked tofu, very thinly sliced

4 green onions, finely sliced

For the dressing /

2 tbsp soy sauce

2 tbsp kecap manis

1 tbsp toasted sesame oil

1 cup vegan vegetable stock

Soak the noodles in a large bowl of freshly boiled water until softened —about 10 minutes—then drain and dress with the tablespoon of soy sauce. Put the onion, ginger, and garlic into a food processor, and pulse to mince. Scrape out the mixture (no need to wash the bowl), and repeat with the beets, walnuts, and cilantro stems.

Heat the canola oil in a non-stick frying pan over a medium flame and, when hot, fry the minced onion paste for 10 minutes, stirring often so it doesn't catch, until it turns a couple of shades darker. Now add the beet mixture, cook for 15 minutes, add the salt and pepper, then cook for 5 minutes more, until deep, rich, and soft, and turn off the heat.

Mix the ingredients for the dressing together, and set aside.

To build the noodle pot, place half the smoked tofu in the base in a single layer, followed by half the noodles (you might need to cut them with kitchen scissors). Top the noodles with two-thirds of the beet mixture, then add another layer each of the remaining tofu and noodles. Top with the remaining beet mixture.

Lightly chop the remaining walnuts and sprinkle over the top with the green onions. Pour over the dressing, close the lid, put the pot on a medium heat, and cook for 12 to 15 minutes. Remove the lid, garnish with chopped cilantro leaves, and serve.

SHIITAKE PHO with crispy leeks   V

There's a whole world of mushrooms out there but the diamond in the rough, in my eyes, is the shiitake. Originally from China, and now grown here, it is sold both fresh and dried, and, when cooked, unleashes an almighty meaty, smoky richness, adding a welcome chewy texture to boot.

In this Hanoi-style pho, the mushroom broth provides a perfect pool for the noodles and spices—cinnamon, star anise, and cloves—to swim in. You could top it with a galaxy of good things, from crispy fried onions to all manner of herbs (fresh mint and cilantro, say), but here I've gone for leeks. This recipe rewards the cook who chops everything in advance.

Serves 4 /

¼ cup canola oil, plus extra
    for shallow-frying

4 shallots, thinly sliced

2 inches ginger, peeled and grated

1 star anise

3 cloves

1 cinnamon stick

2 leeks: 1 sliced, 1 shredded into
    long strips

2 bird's-eye chiles, very
    finely chopped

¾ lb fresh shiitake mushrooms,
    thinly sliced

1 tbsp soy sauce

6 green onions, very finely sliced

8½ cups vegan vegetable stock

optional: salt

7 oz flat rice noodles

a big handful of fresh cilantro leaves,
    shredded

1 lime, quartered

In a large pot (3 quarts or bigger), heat the oil on a medium flame, then fry the shallots for 5 minutes. Stir in the ginger, star anise, cloves, and cinnamon stick, and fry for 5 minutes more, until the mix starts to blacken and turn sticky. Add the finely sliced leek, chiles, and mushrooms, and stir-fry for 8 to 10 minutes, until softened, then add the soy sauce, half the green onions, and the stock. Bring to the boil, turn the heat down to a whisper, and leave to simmer. Check for seasoning: it may well need salt.

Meanwhile, fry the shredded leek. Pour enough oil into a frying pan to come ½ inch up the sides, then heat on a medium flame until very hot. Fry the leek in batches, until crispy and golden, then use a slotted spoon to transfer to a plate lined with paper towels to drain while you fry the rest. Cook the noodles according to the packet instructions and drain.

To serve, distribute the noodles between four bowls, ladle the broth on top, making sure everyone gets a good helping of the vegetables, then scatter with cilantro, the crispy leeks, remaining green onions, and a squeeze of lime.

UDON NOODLES with red cabbage and cauliflower   V

Chewy, fat, and wonderfully slurp-able, udon noodles are my favorite. They're deliciously bouncy and quick to cook, especially the "wok ready" sort. In Japan, they are often added to hot soups, but I've never managed to work out the bowl-to-mouth maneuver without ruining a perfectly good top. I like them best yaki-style: stir-fried with a party of vegetables, and in this instance spiced with curry powder and spiked with lime.

note / Roasting the cabbage brings out its delicious, bitter, caramel notes. The Japanese pink pickled ginger called "beni shoga" is available online, or you can make your own pickled (non-pink) ginger (see page 255).

Serves 4 /

½ a red cabbage (1 lb), cut into 1-inch wedges

1 small cauliflower (1 lb), cut into 1½-inch florets

canola oil

¼ cup soy sauce

8–10 green onions, sliced diagonally into 2-inch pieces

2 cloves of garlic, crushed

3 x 7-oz packages "straight to wok" udon noodles

1 tsp curry powder

2 tbsp mirin

2 tbsp lime juice (from 1½ limes)

To serve /

2 tbsp Japanese pink pickled "beni shoga" ginger

white sesame seeds

Preheat the oven to 475°F.

Put the cabbage on one baking sheet and the cauliflower on another, making sure the latter is in a single layer, so it doesn't steam. In a small bowl, mix 2 tablespoons each of oil and soy sauce, then pour over the cauliflower and cabbage. Pop both sheets into the oven. Roast the cauliflower for 15 minutes, until just tender and blackening, then remove. Roast the cabbage for 20 minutes longer, until burned at the edges but still holding its shape.

Heat 2 tablespoons of oil in a large non-stick frying pan on a medium-high flame. Add the green onions and fry for 2 minutes, until starting to brown but still bright green. Add the garlic and cook for a minute more, stirring occasionally so it doesn't burn.

Add the noodles, toss to coat in the garlicky oil and green onions, then stir in the curry powder and mirin and cook for a minute. Add the cabbage and cauliflower and cook for 2 minutes, until the noodles take on a little color. Add the remaining 2 tablespoons of soy and the lime juice, and toss to coat.

Transfer to four plates or bowls, and sprinkle with the pickled ginger and sesame seeds.

GREEN ONION AND GINGER NOODLES   V

Green onion and ginger are a power couple in the world of ingredients. Although they are ubiquitous throughout much Chinese and Korean cooking, I hadn't understood their transformational power until I started thumbing through David Chang's book *Momofuku*, and came across this green onion and ginger sauce. My discovery has since turned into an addiction and this combination features a little too much in this book—I'm sorry, but I blame David.

note / The sauce keeps for a week in the fridge and can be used on almost anything.

Serves 4 /

14 green onions (½ lb), very
   finely chopped

1½ inches ginger, peeled and very
   finely chopped

⅓ cup canola oil

2½ tsp soy sauce

2 tsp white wine vinegar

¾ tsp salt

14 oz whole wheat noodles

1 tbsp black sesame seeds

Put all the ingredients except for the noodles and sesame seeds into a large bowl and mix together.

Get a medium-sized pan of water up to a rolling boil and, when bubbling, pop in the noodles. Cook for around 3 to 5 minutes, or according to the package instructions, then drain well, tip into the green onion and ginger sauce, and mix.

Distribute between four bowls, sprinkle over the sesame seeds, and serve.

PISTACHIO, PEA, AND MINT SOBA NOODLES

V

A real "welcome to summer dish." All the freshness and lightness that hot weather demands, but with enough in there to keep tummies full.

note / I like to use soba noodles made from buckwheat and wheat as they're easier to handle, but you could use 100 percent buckwheat soba if you prefer. You'll need a food processor for this recipe.

Serves 2 /

½ cup pistachio kernels

1 bird's-eye chile, finely chopped

2 cloves of garlic, finely chopped

1¾ cups frozen petite peas, defrosted

1 cup fresh mint leaves

3 tbsp lime juice (from 2 limes)

3½ tbsp toasted sesame oil

1⅓ tsp salt

7 oz soba noodles

¼ lb snow peas

1¼ cups chopped watercress

Place the pistachios, chile, and garlic into a food processor and process until the pistachios have broken down. Add the peas, mint, lime juice, 3 tablespoons of sesame oil, and the salt, and pulse a few times (don't blend, you don't want soup).

Bring a large saucepan of water to the boil and, when bubbling, drop the soba noodles in. Stir so the noodles don't clump together, and boil according to the package instructions, around 4 to 5 minutes. Drain, refresh briefly under cold water, and set to drain in a sieve over a bowl. Drizzle with the remaining ½ tablespoon of sesame oil, and coat with your fingers to make sure they don't stick.

Set the same saucepan over a low heat and put a couple of table-spoons of water into the pan. When hot, add the snow peas. Stir-fry for 2 minutes, then add the watercress. Stir-fry for a minute until it wilts, then take the pan off the heat.

Place the noodles in a mixing bowl, and add the petite pea mixture, snow peas, and watercress. Mix with your hands and taste for seasoning, adjusting as you see fit, then tip onto a plate to serve.

CARAMELIZED ONION AND CHILE RAMEN

From the outside, Japanese food can seem rigid, steeped in centuries of tradition. But the truth is that it is a story of continual innovation. Ramen, for example, is an adaptation of Chinese wheat noodles and was first introduced to Japan by Chinese immigrants in the early twentieth century. And although there is only one name to describe this soupy noodle dish, there are as many variations of ramen as there are cooks in Japan. My recipe evolved from an unlikely place, taking inspiration from a French onion soup I ate in a cafe in Paris. In my recipe, sticky onions combine with miso, stock, and sake to make a very special-tasting soup.

note / Cooking sake is available in big supermarkets and online. If you can't find it, use Chinese rice wine or dry sherry instead. To veganize this dish, drop the eggs and ensure the stock is suitable for vegans.

Serves 4 /

canola oil

1 large onion, finely sliced

3 cloves of garlic, finely sliced

½ tsp salt

1 bird's-eye chile, finely sliced

6½ cups vegetable stock

2 tbsp cooking sake

1½ tbsp soy sauce

1 tbsp brown rice miso

7 oz ramen noodles

½ lb choy sum, cut into 2½-inch pieces

optional: 4 soy eggs (see page 37) or soft-boiled eggs

optional: chile oil, to serve

In a large, heavy-bottomed saucepan, warm 5 tablespoons of oil over a medium heat. Add the onions, garlic, and salt, stir to coat in the oil, and cook for 8 to 10 minutes, until the onions become translucent. Reduce the heat to its lowest setting and continue to cook for 30 minutes, stirring every 5 minutes. The onions will gradually caramelize and color, eventually breaking down to form a soft, sweet paste. Add the bird's-eye chile and stock, bring to boil, then reduce the heat to a simmer and add the sake, soy sauce, and brown rice miso, stirring well to combine. Check the seasoning and adjust if need be.

Cook your noodles according to the package instructions. Refresh in cold water and stir in a little oil to keep them from sticking together. Finally, bring the broth back to the boil, add the choy sum and cook for 1 to 2 minutes, until tender.

To serve, divide your noodles between four bowls and ladle the broth and greens over the noodles. If you're serving the eggs, halve and pop on top of the bowls, and serve with some chile oil if you like.

FOOD COURT SINGAPORE NOODLES   V

I've been eating Singapore noodles in airport and shopping-mall food courts for years now. They tend to be overcooked and served in a neon oil slick. These noodles are different: spikier in flavor and packed with vegetables.

As with all pan-fried noodle dishes, there are secrets to success. Be sure to prep your ingredients in advance, before you even touch a frying pan. Cook the noodles for a minute less than the package instructions and mix gently to distribute the vegetables through the noodles. Arm yourself with a spaghetti fork or a pair of salad servers and you'll be all right.

note / How long you soak the noodles for will depend on the brand, as they vary.

Serves 2 /

5 oz rice vermicelli noodles

3 tbsp vegetable oil

1 medium red onion, thinly sliced

3 cloves of garlic, crushed

¾ inch ginger, peeled and grated

1 green finger (or serrano) chile, chopped

2 bell peppers (1 red, 1 yellow), thinly sliced

5 oz carrot (1 large), peeled and julienned

a handful of bean sprouts

a handful of green beans, cut lengthways

1 tsp medium curry powder

3 tbsp soy sauce

optional: ½ tsp salt

Fill and boil a kettle. Place the dried noodles in a large heatproof bowl, cover with boiled water, and leave to soften for a minute less than the package instructions specify (it should take 4 to 7 minutes). Drain, refresh under cold running water, drain again, and drizzle with 1 tablespoon of oil to prevent sticking.

Heat the remaining 2 tablespoons of oil in a large frying pan on a high heat and add the onion, garlic, ginger, and chile. Cook for around 5 minutes, stirring regularly so the ginger and garlic don't burn.

Next, add the rest of the vegetables. Cook for 5 minutes, stirring regularly, until all the veg has wilted—this is a comfort dish so you're not really looking for crunch. Finally, add the curry powder, soy sauce, and noodles. Add the salt if need be. Mix well but carefully, until all the noodles are coated and the vegetables are evenly distributed. Serve immediately.

curries

Try to define "curry" and you can't. It is not bound by a technique, or a specific set of ingredients; neither is it limited to certain regions or countries. It's loosely understood to be something cooked in a spiced sauce.

For me, what is more interesting is how the "curry" has traveled, and been interpreted and adapted. Madhur Jaffrey, author of *Ultimate Curry Bible*, is sure that the ribbon of tradition that runs through all curries can be traced back to India. She suggests that when Indian migrants moved out of India, both east and west, as laborers of the British Empire, they took their cooking with them.

It makes sense, then, to start our journey in India. Punjab, in the north of India, is where dairy-loving fiends created India's most popular cheese, paneer. Spinach and paneer is the traditional combination, but in this chapter I've teamed the cheese with kale (see page 124), which grows in my native county, Lincolnshire, in the kind of plumes you might find on a dancing girl's headdress. In this curry, the kale has been blitzed to smithereens and braised in spiced tomatoes until soft.

The north of India is also where you'll find paneer kofta (see page 115): little dumplings made using potatoes and grated paneer. Ordinarily they are deep-fried then served in a rich, creamy sauce, but mine are pan-fried and dished up in a tomato sauce thickened with a handful of cashews.

Moving down the west coast, the next stop is Mysore, the city that smells of sandalwood and yoga mats. This is where I ate my first saagu, a Karnatakan curry thick with coconut and spices. Mine, on page 123, is made with floury potatoes, chard, and coconut, which happily merge into a sauce.

Hop over the border into the state of Kerala and you'll find mild vegetable istoos: vegetables cooked in a ginger, chile, and coconut sauce. While these dishes are not as complex as some curries, they are gentle and elegant, and crucially they don't compromise on flavor (see page 112 for my new potato and green bean istoo).

From Kerala, take a sharp turn right into Tamil Nadu. Between ancient carved temples and silk sari shops, you'll find restaurants serving thakkali kuzhambu, the dish on which my tomato curry (see page 108) is based. In it, pickling spices like mustard, fennel, and cumin seeds come together with tamarind and coconut to form a rich, silken, lip-smacking mass of tomatoes, perfect to scoop up with naan bread.

Sail a few miles across the Arabian Sea to Sri Lanka, and order rice and curry for lunch. Although "curry" is singular, here you'll receive a selection of curries each made from one main ingredient, such as beets, eggplant, pumpkin, or cashew, served alongside a coconut dal (parippu) and perhaps a mallum, a sprightly green dish. See my beet curry with green bean mallum on page 100.

Leave Sri Lanka and travel east to Thailand, where David Thompson, author of the masterpiece *Thai Food*, says that "everyone has a favorite curry." Thompson suggests the curries of the north and central plains (like Thai green curry—see page 120) use more spices because they've been influenced by Indians, while the curries of the south (like massaman curry—see page 114) have been influenced by Muslims and are redolent of cardamom and cumin.

Our last and final stop on this curry journey is Japan, a country with a strong and very different culinary history. Curry became "Japanized" soon after being introduced—not directly by Indians, it would appear, but by British officers. No wonder, then, that the katsu curry bears little resemblance to anything I've eaten in India or elsewhere in the world, though this naturally sweet, spicy, rich sauce has its own magical charm. My version on page 105 is the recipe I make double quantities of, and stow away in the freezer to use on a lazy night.

SRI LANKAN BEET CURRY
with green bean mallum

The greatest souvenir you can take home from Sri Lanka is a love for "rice and curry." Order this for lunch and you'll get a smorgasbord of curries: leek, cashew, beet, jackfruit, pumpkin, and even pineapple. Often, they are heavily spiced with cinnamon, fenugreek, chile, and pepper, then smothered in coconut milk to soften the blow. On the side, you can expect the most fantastic little meal-brighteners, from raw relishes (sambols) made with chile, lime, and coconut, to quickly cooked greens (mallum) and crisp poppadoms. It is one of life's great feasts. This recipe is an introduction to the tradition.

note / Don't let beets' oozing pinkness bully you: just rub a piece of cut potato onto pink fingers, and most stains will disappear.

Serves 4 as a main /

For the curry /

3 tbsp canola oil

6 fresh curry leaves

1 medium red onion, diced

4 cloves of garlic, crushed

1½ green finger (or serrano) chiles, finely chopped

1½ tbsp tomato paste

2 tsp ground cumin

2 lbs raw beets, peeled and cut into ¼-inch slices

1¼ tsp salt

1 x 14-oz can of coconut milk

1 tbsp lime juice

For the green beans /

1 tbsp canola oil

¾ lb green beans, topped, tailed and cut into ½-inch pieces

1 clove of garlic, crushed

½ a green finger (or serrano) chile, very finely chopped

1 tbsp lime juice (from 1 lime)

⅓ tsp salt

3½ tbsp dried shredded coconut

Start with the beet curry. On a medium flame, heat the oil in a wide frying pan for which you have a lid, then fry the curry leaves and leave them to crackle and pop for a minute. Stir in the onion, garlic, and chiles, cook for around 6 minutes, until the onion turns translucent and soft, then add the tomato paste and cumin and cook for another 5 minutes.

Add the beets, salt, and ⅓ cup of water, pop on the lid, and cook for 15 minutes, stirring occasionally; if the curry looks a bit dry, add more water, a tablespoon at a time. Take off the lid, stir in the coconut milk, and simmer for 10 minutes, until the beets are tender and the sauce has reduced. Finally, stir in the lime juice and turn off the heat while you get on with the beans.

In another wide frying pan, heat the oil for the beans on a high flame. Once it's hot, add the beans, stir to coat in the oil, then leave for 3 to 4 minutes, stirring once, until they blister and char. When the beans have got some blackened bits on them, but are still bright green in color, stir in the garlic, chile, lime juice, and salt, and cook for a minute. Finally, add the coconut, stir-fry for a minute, then take off the heat.

LEEK, MUSHROOM, AND KALE SUBJI   V

One of the first lessons I learned in my mother's kitchen was not to waste anything, including the lonely old vegetables at the bottom of the fridge drawer. Even now, years later, Hugh and I take it in turns to breathe new life into whatever's lurking in the fridge in a game we call "fridge bingo." That is how this little subji, an Indian "stir-fry," came about. In it, the sweetness of the leeks, fennel seeds, and peas is grounded and balanced by the earthy mushrooms and kale and cumin seeds. As with nearly all subjis, chapattis and a dollop of (non-dairy) yogurt make for good company.

Serves 4 as a main /

1 tsp cumin seeds

1 tsp fennel seeds

3 tbsp canola oil

1 tsp black mustard seeds

1 medium onion, finely chopped

3 cloves of garlic, finely chopped

1 lb leeks (2 small), trimmed and finely sliced

1½ lbs brown mushrooms, quartered

1¾ tsp red chile powder, such as Kashmiri

½ tsp ground turmeric

1¼ tsp salt

½ lb curly kale, ribs discarded, leaves chopped

1 cup frozen peas, defrosted

Put the cumin and fennel seeds into a mortar, and bash until they're fairly well ground.

Heat the oil in a large frying pan for which you have a lid, then add the ground spices and the mustard seeds and stir-fry for a minute, until the cumin turns a shade darker. Add the onion and cook, stirring often, for around 6 minutes, or until soft, then add the garlic and cook for 2 minutes more.

Add the leeks and cook for around 5 minutes, until they've softened and unravelled, then add the mushrooms. It will seem as if there are too many to fit into the pan, but they will soon cook down.

After 5 minutes, when the mushrooms are juicy, add the chile powder, turmeric, and salt, then stir in the kale and cook for 8 minutes, until tender. Throw in the peas and cook for 2 or 3 minutes more, until they are hot and soft.

Check the subji for chile and salt, adjust to taste, and serve.

EGGPLANT KATSU CURRY
with pickled radishes

Katsu curry is an unlikely-looking thief of the heart, but this mysterious brown concoction is one of Japan's favorite dishes. In my take on it, the curry sauce is made using plenty of naturally sweet vegetables plus a couple of pantry essentials. These modest ingredients come together to form a seductive and silky sauce much greater than the sum of its parts. It's a message to us all never to judge a dish by its color.

note / The sauce freezes well, so feel free to double up when making. You'll need a blender for this recipe.

Serves 4 as a main /

For the radishes /
½ cup finely sliced radishes
½ tsp salt
3 tbsp mirin
3 tbsp white wine vinegar

For the curry /
3 tbsp canola oil
1 medium onion, chopped
½ lb carrots (2–3 medium), peeled and finely diced
½ lb sweet potato (1 medium), peeled and finely diced
4 cloves of garlic, sliced
½ inch ginger, peeled and grated
2 tbsp curry powder
½ cup + 2 tbsp all-purpose flour, divided
2 cups vegan vegetable stock
2 tbsp soy sauce
2 tbsp ketchup
salt
2 small eggplants (1½ lbs), cut lengthways into ¼-inch-thick slices
3½ cups panko breadcrumbs

Preheat the oven to 400°F. Put the radishes into a heatproof bowl, cover with ⅓ cup of just-boiled water, and add the salt, mirin, and vinegar. Stir and leave to cool.

To make the sauce, heat the oil in a lidded frying pan, then fry the onion, carrots, and sweet potato for 10 minutes. Add the garlic and ginger, fry for 2 minutes more, cover, and leave to steam through for 5 minutes. Add the curry powder, mix, then stir in 2 tablespoons of flour until the vegetables are coated. Add the stock little by little, then bring to the boil. Add the soy sauce, ketchup, and ½ teaspoon of salt, then take off the heat. Blend smooth, then return the sauce to the pan.

Line a baking sheet with parchment paper. Put the eggplants on a plate. Put ½ cup of flour on a second, lipped plate, then slowly mix the remaining flour with ¾ cup of water and ½ teaspoon of salt to make a thin paste. Put the panko on a third plate. Cover both sides of each eggplant slice in the flour paste, shaking off any excess, then press into the panko to coat. Lay the coated slices on the prepared sheet and drizzle both sides with oil. Bake for 15 minutes on each side, turn the heat up to 475°F, and cook for 5 to 10 minutes more, until crisp, then take out of the oven.

Just before serving, gently reheat the curry sauce for 5 minutes, adding more water and salt if need be. Put 3 or 4 eggplant slices on each plate, alongside the sauce, then serve with some drained pickled radish, rice, salad, and a sprinkling of black sesame seeds if you like.

SQUASH MALAI KARI   V

I have loosely based this recipe on the Bengali malai kari, a dish made with sweet onions, garam masala, and rich coconut milk. Warming, hearty, and sharpened with a little lime for freshness, it's best eaten with rice or scooped onto the softest naan you can find.

note / If you can't get hold of kabocha, use butternut squash.

Serves 4 as a main /

2½ lbs kabocha squash

canola oil

salt

2 medium red onions, finely chopped

¾ inch ginger, peeled and finely grated

5 cloves of garlic, crushed

¾ cup strained tomatoes

2 tsp ground cumin

¾ tsp ground cinnamon

1¾ tsp red chile powder, such as Kashmiri

1½ tsp garam masala

1 tsp sugar

1½ x 14-oz cans coconut milk

1 lime, cut into wedges

optional: toasted flaked almonds or fresh cilantro, to serve

Preheat the oven to 400°F and line two baking sheets with parchment paper or foil.

Without peeling, cut the squash in half, scoop out and discard the seeds, and cut the flesh into thin crescents, no more than ¾ inch wide. Drizzle with oil, sprinkle with a big pinch of salt, then pop them on the pans in one layer. Bake for 30 to 40 minutes, turning the squash halfway through, until tender and blackening at the edges.

Heat ¼ cup of oil in a deep frying pan over a medium flame and, when hot, add the onions. Cook for 15 minutes until really soft, then add the ginger and garlic. Cook for 3 to 4 minutes, then add the tomato and cook for a further 6 minutes, until rich and paste-like. Add 1½ teaspoons of salt, the spices, and the teaspoon of sugar, stir to mix, then add the coconut milk. Mix well and heat through until it's thick and bubbling. Taste, squeeze in a little lime, and taste again, adjusting the salt, sugar, or lime juice as you wish.

To serve, pour the sauce onto each plate and top with a few wedges of squash. Sprinkle over some toasted almonds or fresh cilantro if you like, and serve with naan bread or rice.

TOMATO CURRY

There are just a few Indian dishes that truly celebrate the tomato, such as Keralan tomato fry and Gujarati sev tameta nu shaak (a sweet and sour tomato curry), but it's thakkali kuzhambu, from Tamil Nadu, on which this recipe is (very) loosely based. The sweetness and acidity of tomatoes is married to classic pickling spices, then tempered with curry leaves, tamarind, and coconut: the ingredients that define South Indian cooking. This dish has a magic moment when all the water in the coconut milk evaporates to render the oil, leaving you with a silky, luxurious heap of deliciousness that's perfect for scooping up with naan bread or mixing into hot rice.

note / You'll need two large frying pans for this recipe.

Serves 4 as a main /

1¼ tsp fennel seeds

1¼ tsp black mustard seeds

1¼ tsp cumin seeds

1¼ tsp coriander seeds

canola oil

2 medium onions, halved and finely sliced

1¼ tsp salt

8 fresh curry leaves, plus extra to garnish if you like

2½ lbs small ripe tomatoes in a mix of colors

1½ green finger (or serrano) chiles, very finely chopped

4 cloves of garlic, crushed

2½ tsp tamarind paste

1 x 14-oz can of coconut milk

Heat a large frying pan on a medium flame and, when hot, toast the fennel, mustard, cumin, and coriander seeds for a minute or two, shaking the pan every few seconds, until the coriander seeds turn golden (coriander always takes first). Tip the seeds into a mortar and bash until fairly well ground.

Heat ¼ cup of oil in the same pan and, when hot, return the ground spices with the onions, salt, and curry leaves. Fry for 10 to 12 minutes, until the onions are golden and crisp-edged. Meanwhile, cut the tomatoes in half.

Add the chiles and garlic to the pan and cook, stirring, for 2 minutes. Then add the tamarind and coconut milk, stir, and transfer half the mixture into your second large frying pan.

Divide the tomatoes between both pans, so they sit in one layer. Set both pans on a medium heat and cook for 20 to 25 minutes without stirring: you want the tomatoes to keep their shape while driving off the water in the coconut milk. You'll know there's none left when you can see oil at the sides of the pan. (The curry won't be dry: the tomatoes contain a lot of juice, which will come out while they're resting.) Now tip the contents of the second pan gently back into the first.

If you'd like to add a final bit of pizazz, heat a little oil in a saucepan and, when hot, drop in a handful of extra curry leaves. Let them crackle and crisp, then take off the heat and pour over the tomatoes. Serve with naan or rice.

ROASTED PANEER ALOO GOBI

This was an experiment in the early days of parenthood to see if a curry could be cooked in the oven. In short: it can. But I learned that roasting spices can be challenging, as the dry heat often burns them or dulls the flavors. One way to counter this is to increase the amount of spice you use and add them to a wet sauce, so they don't frazzle away. The second is to wake up the spices after cooking with a little lemon juice.

Serves 4 (or 2, two nights running) /

⅓ cup canola oil

2½ tsp ground coriander

2½ tsp ground cumin

2 tsp red chile powder, such as Kashmiri

½ tsp garam masala

1½ tsp salt

4 cloves of garlic, crushed

¾ inch ginger, peeled and grated

2 medium red onions, halved and cut into ½-inch wedges

½ lb paneer, cut into ¾-inch cubes

1⅓ lbs cauliflower (1 medium), broken into florets

¾ lb Russet potatoes, peeled and cut into ¾-inch cubes

1 lb ripe tomatoes, roughly chopped

chopped fresh cilantro and lemon wedges, to serve

Preheat the oven to 400°F and line two large sheet pans with foil.

Next, make the marinade. In a small bowl mix the oil, ground coriander, cumin, chile powder, garam masala, salt, garlic, and ginger, and set aside.

Place the onions and paneer on one sheet pan, and the cauliflower and potatoes on the other. Pour an equal amount of the dressing over both sheet pans, making sure you scrape every last bit out of the bowl, and rub everything with your hands, making sure all the vegetables are covered. Place the onion and paneer sheet pan at the top of the oven, and the cauliflower in the middle. Roast for 25 minutes, or until the cauliflower and potatoes are tender and blackening, then remove both sheet pans. Cover the cauliflower and potato sheet pan with foil to keep warm.

Add the chopped tomatoes to the onion and paneer sheet pan and return to the oven for another 15 minutes. After this time, remove from the oven and tip the potatoes and cauliflower into the tomato sheet pan, gently mix, and taste, adding a little more salt if you like.

Sprinkle with chopped cilantro, squeeze over the lemon, and serve alongside yogurt and naan breads.

NEW POTATO AND GREEN BEAN ISTOO

Black pepper, once a highly prized spice for which kingdoms fell and men died, originates in India's Malabar coast, where it's one of the main spices of the local cuisine. When used as more than just a seasoning, as in this istoo (a corruption of "stew"), pepper adds a gentle heat, unlike the sharp hit you get from fresh chiles. The result is one of the most elegant curries I've come across in all my travels across India.

This curry is a variation on one in my book *Fresh India*, and really begs to be served with sweet, roasted tamarind shallots (see page 244), which can be cooked in the oven at the same time as the istoo. If you've no time or inclination to make the shallots, an invigorating eggplant (brinjal) pickle would do nicely.

Serves 4 as part of a bigger spread /

2 tbsp canola oil

10 fresh curry leaves

1½ inch cinnamon stick, broken in two

1 medium onion, sliced

1 inch ginger, peeled and finely grated

4 cloves of garlic, crushed

1 green finger (or serrano) chile, slit

1½ lbs small new potatoes, quartered

1 tsp each salt and ground black pepper

1 x 14-oz can of coconut milk

½ lb green beans, trimmed and halved crosswise

In a casserole dish for which you have a lid, heat the oil for the istoo on a medium flame and, once hot, add the curry leaves, cinnamon stick, and onion. Cook for 8 to 10 minutes, until the onion is as soft as possible without coloring, then stir in the ginger, garlic, and chile, and cook for 2 minutes.

Add the potatoes, salt, and pepper, stir in the coconut milk, then fill the empty can with ⅓ cup of water, swirl it around, and add to the casserole—you want just to cover the potatoes, so add more water, if need be. Bring to the boil on a medium heat, then turn the heat down and simmer for 10 minutes.

Add the beans, cover with the lid, and simmer until both the beans and potatoes are tender—around 5 to 6 minutes (longer, if you prefer your beans soft).

Serve with hot basmati rice, or, if you're able to find them in an Indian shop, fermented coconut appam pancakes.

SWEET POTATO AND EGGPLANT MASSAMAN CURRY

V

Growing up, "something from the cupboard" became a regular and comforting option—especially in deep winter, when going out to buy something fresh meant de-icing our old Nissan Bluebird that was so full of holes, the eye-stinging wind would freeze our fingers blue. We spent a lot of time with our noses in the kitchen drawers, wondering how best to use cans of this and that. These days, I have a more global pantry and it is as easy to whip up a spaghetti as it is this massaman curry. A massaman curry has many variations, but it's usually sweet, sour with tamarind, and made using spices, peanuts, and coconut; it also often features a starchy vegetable such as potato or sweet potato. Though ordinarily it's complex to make, I've taken liberties by using as many pantry ingredients as possible.

note / You'll need a blender for this recipe. You can order galangal paste online. Fresh galangal is available at Asian supermarkets—just grate it like ginger to make a paste.

Serves 4 /

For the paste /

5 bird's-eye chiles

2 shallots, roughly chopped

2 lemongrass stalks, bottom 2 inches only, roughly chopped

1 cup cilantro (leaves and stems), roughly chopped

⅓ cup smooth peanut butter

1½ tsp ground cumin

¾ tsp ground cinnamon

½ tsp ground cloves

1½ tbsp galangal paste

1½ tbsp tamarind paste

2½ tsp sugar

1½ tsp salt

For the curry /

2 x 14-oz cans of coconut milk

1 lb eggplant (1 medium), cut into ¾-inch x ¾-inch chunks

2 lbs sweet potatoes (4 medium), peeled and cut into 1-inch x 1-inch chunks

a handful of dried coconut slices, to garnish

Put all the ingredients for the paste into a blender, reserving a handful of cilantro leaves to garnish the finished dish. Add ⅓ cup of water and blitz.

Put a large pan for which you have a lid on a medium heat and, once hot, fry the paste, stirring constantly, for 5 minutes, until dark and glossy; take care it doesn't catch and burn. Add the coconut milk little by little, stirring it in as you go, then throw in the eggplant and bring the lot up to a bubble. Add the sweet potatoes, cover the pan, turn the heat down to a whisper, and leave to cook for 20 minutes, until the eggplant has collapsed and the sweet potatoes are very tender.

While the curry is cooking, toast the coconut slices. Put a small frying pan on a medium flame and, once hot, toast the coconut for a couple of minutes, until golden brown on both sides.

To serve, transfer the curry to a serving bowl, scatter the reserved cilantro leaves and coconut slices on top, and serve with plain rice.

PANEER KOFTA
with a tomato and cashew sauce

When friends travel to India, they come back and ask me for a recipe for this dish, also known as malai kofta. The kofta are compact little balls of joy made from paneer and potato, spiced with pepper, chile, and ginger. They are lovely by themselves or submerged in a warm hug of a sauce made from tomatoes and sweet creamy cashews.

note / Kasuri methi are dried fenugreek leaves that add a pungent, earthy flavor. They're found in boxes in Indian grocery stores. You'll need a blender for this recipe.

Serves 4 as a main /

For the tomato and cashew sauce /

½ cup unsalted cashews

3 tbsp canola oil

1 medium onion, chopped

4 cloves of garlic, crushed

2 x 14-oz cans of petite diced tomatoes

1½ tsp red chile powder, such as Kashmiri

1 tsp garam masala

½ tsp ground cinnamon

1 tsp salt

optional: 1 tsp kasuri methi, plus more to decorate

For the kofta /

1 lb Russet potatoes, peeled, boiled and cooled

8 oz paneer, grated

1 green finger (or serrano) chile, finely chopped

½ inch ginger, peeled and grated

1 tsp ground black pepper

1 tsp salt

canola oil

First, make the tomato and cashew sauce. Place the cashews in a small heatproof bowl, pour over just-boiled water to cover, and leave to soak for 10 minutes. Drain, then blend the cashews into a paste with 5 tablespoons of water (add a little extra water if needed).

Put the oil into a frying pan over a medium heat and, when hot, add the onion. Cook for 10 minutes, until soft, then add the garlic. Cook for 2 minutes, then add the petite diced tomatoes and all their juices to the pan, mix well, and leave to cook for 10 minutes, until the tomatoes turn paste-like and start to release oil back into the pan. Add the chile powder, garam masala, cinnamon, salt, and the cashew paste to the pan, along with the kasuri methi, if using. Cook for a further 5 minutes, loosening with water if need be to make the consistency saucier, then take off the heat while you make the kofta.

Grate the cooled boiled potatoes and add to a bowl with the paneer, green chile, ginger, pepper, and salt. Mix well with your hands and form into 12 patties (1 inch thick by 2 inches wide). Put 2 tablespoons of oil into a frying pan and, when hot, fry the patties in batches for 2 minutes on each side until a golden crust has formed, then remove to a plate.

Once all the koftas are ready, heat up the sauce and pop the koftas in to warm up. Sprinkle over some more kasuri methi if using, and serve hot with naan bread.

EGGPLANT POLLICHATTU

Indian food has a north–south divide. While food from the north is (in general) slow, heavy, and often a shade of red or brown, food from the south is faster, fresher, and more brightly flavored. It's long been a mystery to me why food from the north has tended to dominate our high streets. This Keralan dish, traditionally cooked in a banana leaf, is a wonderful introduction to the food of South India. Wrapping the eggplant in parchment paper part bakes and part steams it, making it wonderfully creamy and soft. This means a crunchy salad would sit nicely alongside.

note / You'll need four sheets of parchment paper cut into 16-inch x 16-inch squares and kitchen string or regular string soaked in cold water.

Serves 4 as a main /

3 tbsp coconut oil

20 fresh curry leaves

1 lb shallots (5 large), finely sliced

5 cloves of garlic, finely sliced

1 inch ginger, peeled and grated

2 green finger (or serrano) chiles, finely chopped

1 lb ripe tomatoes, roughly chopped

1 tbsp tamarind paste

⅓ cup coconut cream

½ tsp ground turmeric

1 tsp salt

2 lbs eggplants (3 small)

Preheat the oven to 425°F.

Heat the coconut oil in a large frying pan over a medium flame, then add the curry leaves and leave them to crackle and crisp for a minute. Add the shallots and cook for 8 minutes, until they are translucent and just starting to brown, then add the garlic, ginger, and chiles. Cook for 3 or 4 minutes, until the scent of garlic and ginger has filled the kitchen, then add the tomatoes. Cook for 4 minutes, until the tomatoes have broken down, then add the tamarind paste, coconut cream, turmeric, and salt. Simmer together for 15 minutes, until you have a deep ocher sauce that is thick enough to spread (i.e. not too runny). Take off the heat and leave to cool.

Remove the stems from the eggplants and cut lengthways into ½-inch-thick slices, to get 16 slices if you can, then separate the eggplant slices into 4 portions. Roughly divide the sauce in the pan into 4 portions, too.

Put a slice of eggplant in the middle of each piece of parchment paper, add a spoonful of sauce, and add another slice. Repeat until you have a four-slice sandwich. Bring the parchment paper up at either side of the eggplant and fold it over so the eggplant is encased. Do the same with the ends, so that you have a neat package. Tie with string so that it looks like a present. Put this package on a baking sheet and repeat with the rest of your eggplant portions until you have 4 identical packages. Put these in the oven and cook for 45 minutes, or until the eggplant is tender (prick a package with a sharp knife to check). Serve with a chopped salad and some naan or flatbread.

THAI GREEN CURRY with eggplant, zucchini, and snow peas

V

Thai restaurants have long set up shop in some of my favorite pubs in London. This phenomenon started in the mid 1980s at the Churchill Arms in Kensington, and many other pubs soon followed suit. As a result, the Thai green curry has been with me through thick and thin since I moved to London in my twenties. Through birthdays and break-ups, it has helped to bolster proceedings and to soften blows. It strikes a perfect balance of fresh green chile heat and sweet, calm coconut, and in my eyes has no other competitor for comfort.

note / I've used both broccoli and snow peas here, but you could just use one. You'll need a blender for this recipe.

Serves 4 as a main /

For the paste /

4 green finger (or serrano) chiles, roughly chopped

3 lemongrass stalks, bottom 2 inches only, roughly chopped

4 fat cloves of garlic, roughly chopped

1½ tbsp galangal paste, drained

¾ inch ginger, peeled and chopped

1½ tsp salt

¼ tsp ground black pepper

8 Makrut lime leaves or 1 tsp lime zest

1 tsp cumin seeds

½ tsp ground turmeric

canola oil

For the curry /

2 small eggplants (1½ lbs), cut into ¾-inch cubes

2 medium zucchini (1 lb), cut into ¾-inch cubes

1 x 14-oz can of coconut milk

1½ tsp sugar

¼ lb broccoli

¼ lb snow peas

Put all the paste ingredients into a blender, along with 2 tablespoons of canola oil and 2 tablespoons of water, and blend as smooth as possible. (Add a little more oil and water if you need to.)

Over a medium-high heat, put 2 tablespoons of oil into a large frying pan for which you have a lid and, when hot, add the eggplant in a single layer (you may need to fry them in a couple of batches). Fry for around 8 minutes, turning every 2 minutes, or until tender—browning on the outside and softening inside—then transfer to a plate.

Drizzle more oil into the hot pan and cook the zucchini for 4 minutes, turning after 2 minutes, or until almost tender and browning on the outside. Transfer to another plate.

Put a tablespoon of oil into the same pan and, when hot, add the paste. Stir-fry for 4 minutes, then slowly add the coconut milk and ¾ cup of water, and mix. When the milk starts to bubble, add the sugar, cooked vegetables, broccoli, and snow peas, and simmer for 6 minutes, or until all the vegetables are tender, then take off the heat. Serve in bowls with freshly boiled or steamed jasmine rice alongside.

NEW POTATO, CHARD, AND COCONUT CURRY

V

This dish started life in Karnataka, on the west coast of India. It's a spin on saagu, a curry of whatever vegetables happen to be in season, cooked gently in a soothing, spiced coconut sauce: filling enough to be restorative, quick enough to cook midweek, and light enough to be good company on a summer's night.

note / If you don't have a blender, chop the garlic, ginger, and chiles as finely as your fingers and knives will allow, and cook for an extra 5 minutes.

Serves 4 as a main /

1 tsp cumin seeds

3 cloves of garlic

1 inch ginger, peeled and roughly chopped

2 green finger (or serrano) chiles, roughly chopped

¼ cup dried shredded coconut

1 x 14-oz can of coconut milk

3 tbsp canola oil

1 medium onion, halved and thinly sliced

1½ lbs new potatoes, halved lengthways

1½ tsp garam masala

½ tsp ground turmeric

1 tsp salt

½ lb rainbow chard, stems chopped, leaves shredded

1⅔ cups frozen peas, defrosted

Put the cumin, garlic, ginger, chiles, and shredded coconut into a blender with just enough of the coconut milk to blitz everything to a smooth paste. Add the rest of the coconut milk and lightly pulse (over-mixing might split it) to a sauce-like consistency.

In a wide frying pan for which you have a lid, heat the oil over a medium flame and fry the onion for 5 minutes, until translucent. Add the potatoes cut side down and fry for around 10 minutes, until they are lightly golden brown and the onions are soft, dark, and sticky.

Stir in the garam masala, turmeric, and salt, then add the coconut sauce and bring up to a gentle bubble. Add the chard stems, cover, and cook for 5 minutes. Add the leaves and the peas, cover again, and simmer for a final 5 minutes, until the chard stems, peas, and potatoes are tender and the leaves have wilted. Serve with basmati rice or chapattis and a fiery pickle on the side.

PANEER, TOMATO, AND KALE SAAG

For years, I was in kale purgatory. I wanted to love it but I just couldn't. Each bite tasted like a hedge: stubborn and spiky. But as voices around the world mounted in support of kale, so did my desire to find a way to make the unlovable lovable. It took much experimentation, but finally the result is this. It's a recipe for 4 people, but I could easily eat the whole thing myself. It stands up as a "saag" by itself, but is all the better for some fried paneer.

note / You'll need a food processor for this curry.

Serves 4 as a main /

1 lb curly kale, ribs discarded, leaves roughly chopped

canola oil

1 lb paneer, cut into ¾-inch cubes

2 medium onions, finely chopped

¾ inch ginger, peeled and grated

4 cloves of garlic, crushed

2 green finger (or serrano) chiles, finely chopped

1 x 14-oz can of petite diced tomatoes

1½ tsp ground coriander

1½ tsp ground cumin

½ tsp ground turmeric

1½ tsp salt

1 tsp agave syrup

1 x 14-oz can of coconut milk

Pop the kale into the food processor and whizz into little bits. You'll probably need to do this in two batches and stop halfway through each to push down the bigger bits with a spatula or spoon. Transfer to a big bowl and leave to one side.

On a medium flame, heat 2 tablespoons of oil in a large non-stick frying pan for which you have a lid and, when hot, add the paneer cubes. Fry for a couple of minutes on each side, until they are golden all over, then remove to a plate.

Put another 2 tablespoons of oil into the same pan and place back over a medium heat. When hot, add the onions and cook for 10 minutes until soft and sweet, then add the ginger, garlic, and chiles. Cook for 5 minutes, then add the tomatoes. Cook the tomatoes, stirring every now and then, for 8 minutes, until they've reduced to a paste, then add the coriander, cumin, turmeric, salt, and agave syrup, and mix well.

Add the kale to the pan in batches, stirring between each handful. It may seem like there is too much kale at first, but it will wilt quickly. Add the coconut milk, stir, and cover with the lid. Leave to cook over a low heat for 15 minutes, then put the paneer back into the pan and cook for another 10 minutes. If the saag seems dry at any point, add a little water, a couple of tablespoons at a time.

Taste to check that the flavors have blended and the kale is tender before you take it off the heat, and serve with hot whole grain chapattis or fluffy naan bread.

rice

As one of life's pleasures, there's nothing like the steam that hits the face when you lift the lid of a freshly cooked batch of rice. It's like a portal to a tropical rainforest.

Rice is the staple food and major crop of many countries in East Asia, and although there are perhaps 400,000 varieties worldwide, only a fraction of these are available to us in stores. On the next few pages you'll find a guide to the rice I use in this chapter, and how to handle and cook it.

PORTION SIZE

Rice portions can vary depending on appetite and also what it is being eaten with. But as a rough guide, I'd recommend anywhere between ⅓ cup and ½ cup of rice per person.

LONG-GRAIN AND MEDIUM-GRAIN RICE

Basmati and wild + basmati rice

The longest grain of them all is my beloved basmati. This is India's status rice, grown in the paddy fields of the Himalayas. But it's also the rice that makes up my bones and for me smells like home. Steam-cook it in stock, like a pilau, and it will obligingly absorb the surrounding flavors. Basmati is often mixed with wild rice, which gives a great contrast between the soft fluffy basmati and firm, nutty wild. It makes the rice more robust too, making it easier to use it as a base to mix other flavors into, without breaking the grains.

To cook 1¾ cups—enough for 4

Wash/soak: For fluffy basmati, get rid of the excess starch with a wash and soak. Place it in a bowl, cover with water, and agitate with your hands until the water turns cloudy. Drain and repeat until the water is clear, then soak the rice for 10 minutes in hand-hot water, or 20 minutes in cold water, then drain again.

To boil: Place the drained rice in a pan and cover with plenty of freshly boiled water. Bring back up to the boil, simmer for 10 to 12 minutes or until tender, then drain. Cover with a clean kitchen towel and leave to rest for 5 to 10 minutes.

To steam: Place the drained rice in a lidded saucepan with 2½ cups of freshly boiled water. Bring to the boil, then place the lid on and turn the heat down to a whisper. Cook for 10 minutes, then take off the heat and leave to steam with the lid on for a further 10 minutes.

VENERE NERO

STICKY

SUSHI

JASMINE

WILD + BASMATI

BASMATI

Jasmine rice

Jasmine rice is Thailand's long-grain variety, poetically named for its creamy white color rather than its scent (in fact it smells faintly like popcorn when it cooks). This is a great everyday rice as it does not need soaking. You can just wash it and throw it straight into a pan—as such, it's perfect for weeknight dinners.

To cook 1¾ cups—enough for 4

Wash/soak: Place the rice in a sieve and rinse under a cold tap until the water runs clear, then drain.

To boil: Place the drained rice in a pan and cover with plenty of freshly boiled water. Bring back up to boil, simmer for 15 minutes or until tender, then drain. Cover with a clean kitchen towel and leave to rest for 5 to 10 minutes.

To steam: Place the drained rice in a lidded pan with 2½ cups of freshly boiled water. Bring to the boil, place the lid on, then turn the heat down to a whisper. Cook for 15 minutes, then take off the heat and leave to steam with the lid on for a further 5 to 10 minutes.

Venere nero rice

The only medium-grain rice I use in this book, and a relatively new kid on the block. Black rice was once rare and forbidden to all but the Chinese aristocracy as it was thought to ensure longevity. But in the 1990s it was crossed with an Italian risotto rice to create a delightfully firm, chewy, and nutty rice unlike any other rice I've tasted before. It's since become available online. I use it in my forbidden rice salad (see page 47) and in my congee (see page 157), the hot rice porridge eaten for breakfast in China.

To cook 1¾ cups—enough for 4

Wash/soak: No need to wash or soak.

To cook: Place in a pan and cover with plenty of cold water. Bring to the boil, simmer for 18 minutes or until tender, then drain (if cooking congee, follow the instructions on page 157). Cover with a clean kitchen towel and leave to rest for 5 to 10 minutes.

SHORT-GRAIN RICE

Short-grain and sushi rice

Short-grain rice is popular in Korea, Thailand, and Japan. The starch in these grains makes them cling on tightly to one another when cooked, making them perfect for eating with chopsticks. The Korean bibimbap (see page 148) is a great introduction to a dish made with short-grain or sushi rice (outside of sushi).

To cook 1¾ cups—enough for 4

Wash/soak: Place the rice in a medium-sized lidded pan and cover with lukewarm water. Agitate with your hand until the water turns cloudy. Drain and repeat, until the water runs clear. Cover with warm water and leave to soak for 5 minutes, then drain again.

To cook: Place the drained rice back into the pan with 1⅔ cups of cold water. Put the lid on, bring to the boil, then turn the heat down to a whisper and cook for 10 minutes. Take off the heat and leave to steam with the lid on for a further 10 minutes.

Thai sticky (or glutinous) rice

Thai sticky rice is the stickiest of all, and is usually served in one gloriously chewy clump in Thai restaurants. It's a good idea to season this rice as it cooks, as it is too sticky to season afterwards. See my eggplant larb (page 147) for a great sticky rice recipe.

To cook 1¾ cups—enough for 4

Wash/soak: Place the rice in a sieve and rinse it well under the cold tap, then drain. Cover the rice with cold water and leave to soak for 20 minutes, then drain again.

To cook: Put the drained rice in a lidded pan, cover with 2¼ cups of cold water, and add ½ teaspoon of salt. Bring to the boil, then turn the heat down to its lowest setting and simmer for 15 minutes, until all the water has evaporated and the rice is cooked. Cover with the lid and leave to stand for at least 10 minutes.

BRUSSELS SPROUT NASI GORENG   V

Sometimes, all you really want is something with the sort of delicious, spot-hitting taste that I used to think only good takeout could provide—until I accidentally re-created it while writing this recipe. It's fried rice, but not as you know it: smothered in umami-ific sauces and topped with shredded, marinated Brussels sprouts for crunch and zing. All the joy of takeout, but without the wait or delivery charge.

note / Kecap manis is a sweet Indonesian soy sauce that can be found in larger supermarkets, online, and in South East Asian food shops (to make your own, see page 256). You can deseed the chiles if you prefer less heat. I cut the Brussels sprouts by hand, but you could use the fine slicing attachment on a food processor.

Serves 4 as a main /

1¾ cups jasmine rice

3 tbsp canola oil

1 medium red onion, chopped

4 cloves of garlic, crushed

3 bird's-eye chiles, very
   finely chopped

1¾ lbs Brussels sprouts, very
   finely sliced

2 tbsp tomato paste

2 tbsp kecap manis

1¼ tsp salt, plus extra to taste

2 tbsp soy sauce

2 tbsp white wine vinegar

2 tbsp toasted sesame oil

1 tsp sugar

Place the rice in a sieve and rinse under a cold tap until the water runs clear. Tip the rice into a pan, add 2½ cups of freshly boiled water, and bring to the boil. Place the lid on, then turn the heat down to a whisper and cook for 15 minutes. Take off the heat and leave to steam with the lid on.

To cook the nasi goreng base, heat the canola oil in a large frying pan on a medium flame and fry the onion, stirring, for 5 minutes. Add the garlic and two-thirds of the chopped chiles, cook for 2 minutes more, then add all but two large handfuls of the Brussels sprouts. Fry for 8 minutes, leaving them undisturbed for a couple of minutes at a time, so they get some color on them. Then stir in the tomato paste, kecap manis, salt, and a tablespoon each of soy sauce and vinegar. Cook for another 5 minutes, then take off the heat.

To make the marinated Brussels sprouts, put the remaining raw sliced Brussels sprouts into a bowl with 1 tablespoon of soy sauce, 1 tablespoon of vinegar, the sesame oil, sugar, and the remaining chopped chiles. Mix very well and set aside.

To finish the nasi goreng, put the Brussels sprouts and onion pan on a medium heat and gently scoop in the steamed rice, folding it in until well mixed. Heat through, stirring gently, for 5 minutes, until the rice is nice and hot, and season with salt to taste. Transfer to a big platter, scatter the marinated Brussels sprouts over the top, and serve.

rice

COCONUT RICE with eggplant and pickled cucumber

One of the reasons I live in London is that I can travel anywhere in the world through the city's food. Within a 10-minute walk, I could be eating hand-pulled noodles from the northern Chinese province of Xinjiang, smoky eggplant cooked over coals by Anatolian Turks, or Nigerian fried yam. Even if I've not been to the country in question, a dish can transport me there instantly. This is what happened when I ate my first Malaysian nasi lemak. I have tried to re-create these flavors here, and while I can't claim it has any authenticity, I hope it will transport you as it did me.

Serves 4 as a main /

For the pickles /

½ a cucumber

2 tbsp lemon juice

¼ tsp salt

¾ tsp sugar

½ a bird's-eye chile, very finely chopped

For the rice /

1¾ cups jasmine rice

1¼ cups coconut milk (the rest of the can goes into the eggplant)

¼ tsp salt

For the eggplant /

3 tbsp canola oil

1 medium red onion, halved and thinly sliced

3 cloves of garlic, crushed

1½ bird's-eye chiles, very finely chopped

2¼ lbs eggplant (2 medium), cut into slices then into ½-inch-thick batons

⅓ cup coconut milk

1 tbsp tamarind paste

1 tbsp soy sauce

¼ tsp salt

½ tsp sugar

a handful of salted peanuts, crushed

First, make the pickles. Cut the cucumber in half lengthways, scoop out and discard the seeds, then finely dice the flesh. Put into a bowl with the lemon juice, salt, sugar, and chile, and mix to combine.

Place the rice in a sieve and rinse under a cold tap until the water runs clear. Scoop into a saucepan for which you have a lid, with 1¼ cups of coconut milk, 1 cup of water, and salt, bring to the boil, then cover the pan and turn the heat down to a whisper. Cook for 15 minutes, then take off the heat and leave to steam with the lid on.

In a lidded frying pan, heat the oil on a high flame, then fry the onion, stirring, for about 8 minutes, until soft and golden. Add the garlic and chiles, cook for a couple of minutes more, then stir in the eggplant. Add 3 tablespoons of water, clap on the lid, and leave to cook, stirring every now and then; if it starts looking too dry, add a tablespoon of water. After about 15 minutes, when the eggplant is starting to brown and has reduced in volume, add the ⅓ cup of coconut milk, the tamarind, soy sauce, salt, and the sugar. Cook until the liquid evaporates, then take off the heat.

To serve, pile the eggplant on top of the rice, scatter some drained cucumber pickles on top, and finish with a sprinkling of peanuts.

rice

SPRING PILAU with asparagus, fennel, and pea

V

In the cut-and-thrust of spring, it can feel that all the vegetables have turned up to the party at once. So the question is not so much which one to eat, but how to hang a few together so they make sense on the same plate. In this simple pilau, the fennel softens and melts into the background, joining the onions and garlic to form a deep base flavor, while the asparagus, peas, fava beans, and herbs take a front seat, to keep things light, fresh, and sweet.

note / Although I prefer homemade, I like high-quality storebought garam masalas, too. Whichever you use, make sure it's fresh and doesn't taste like sawdust. Feel free to add more peas and skip the fava beans if you prefer.

Serves 4 as a main /

1¾ cups basmati rice

2½ cups vegan vegetable stock

3 tbsp canola oil

2 medium red onions, finely sliced

4 cloves of garlic, crushed

2 green finger (or serrano) chiles, very finely sliced

1 fennel bulb, trimmed and thinly sliced

½ lb asparagus, trimmed, cut into 1½-inch pieces

1⅓ cups defrosted frozen peas, or a mix of fresh peas and fava beans

1½ tsp ground cumin

1½ tsp garam masala

¾ tsp salt

a big handful of fresh mint leaves

a big handful of fresh dill

1 lemon, cut into wedges, to serve

Wash the rice in a few changes of cold water until it runs clear, then leave to soak in cold water for 20 minutes. Drain the rice, put into a large lidded saucepan, and pour over the stock. Bring to the boil, then cover the pan, turn the heat down to a whisper, and leave to cook for 10 to 12 minutes. Take off the heat and leave the rice, still covered, to steam through until needed.

Meanwhile, heat the oil in a large, lidded pan on a medium flame. Once hot, add the onions and cook for 6 to 8 minutes, until translucent and softening but not yet colored. Add the garlic and chiles, cook for another 2 minutes, then stir in the fennel and a couple of tablespoons of water, and cover the pan. Leave to cook for 8 minutes, until soft, then add the asparagus, peas, fava beans, cumin, garam masala, and salt. Stir, cover again, cook for 3 to 5 minutes more, then take off the heat.

Finely chop the herbs and fold them and the rice into the vegetable mixture—you might need to break up any clumps of rice delicately with your hands—then transfer to a serving dish and serve with wedges of lemon on the side.

SUMMER PILAU
with tomato, coconut, and cashews

V

Tomatoes work in different ways in this recipe: they create a wonderful sauce with the coconut milk, which is used to flavor and cook the rice, and then they float to the top to decorate the dish. The end result is a dish delicious enough to stand on its own feet without the need for anything else and (as a side benefit) it uses just a single pan. You'll need a wide frying pan with a tight-fitting lid.

note / Curry leaves add a lovely citrus and smoke flavor to the rice but can be tricky to find unless you live near an Asian supermarket. If you can't find them, leave them out.

Serves 4 as a main /

1¾ cups basmati rice

2 tbsp canola oil

12 fresh curry leaves

1½ inches cinnamon stick

1 medium onion, finely sliced

4 cloves of garlic, crushed

1 green finger (or serrano) chile,
   finely sliced

½ cup unsalted cashews

1 lb grape tomatoes, halved

1 x 14-oz can of coconut milk

1¾ tsp salt

Wash the rice in a few changes of cold water until the water runs clear, then leave to soak in plenty of cold water.

Meanwhile, heat the oil in a wide frying pan and add the curry leaves and cinnamon stick. Stir-fry for a minute, then add the onion and cook for around 10 to 12 minutes, until it starts to turn golden brown and is soft enough to cut with a wooden spoon. Add the garlic, chile, and cashews, and cook for a couple of minutes, then add the tomatoes and pop the lid on. Cook for around 8 minutes, until the tomatoes are soft and jammy around the edges.

Drain the rice, add it to the pan, and stir to combine. Add the coconut milk, scant 1 cup of water, and the salt. Stir again and bring the mixture to the boil, then pop the lid on, turn the heat down to a whisper, and cook for a further 15 minutes. Don't be tempted to lift the lid as the steam is key to cooking the rice. Once the 15 minutes is up, take off the heat and keep the lid on for a further 10 minutes to let the rice rest before eating. Serve alongside a fresh green salad.

AUTUMN PILAU with squash, lacinato kale, and smoked garlic

V

In this autumnal pilau I've used two of the season's finest vegetables—buttery squash and earthy plumes of lacinato kale—alongside smoked garlic, which adds a glorious and timely bonfirey-ness to proceedings.

note / If you can't find smoked garlic, use raw garlic and replace the salt in the recipe with smoked salt.

Serves 4 as a main /

1⅔ cups basmati rice

2½ lbs squash, halved, deseeded, and cut into ½-inch half-moons

¼ cup + 1 tbsp canola oil

salt and ground black pepper

3 medium onions, thinly sliced

4 cloves of smoked garlic, very thinly sliced

1½ tsp ground cumin

1½ tsp garam masala

½ tsp ground turmeric

2 green finger (or serrano) chiles, finely chopped

½ cup packed cilantro leaves and stems, finely chopped

1 lb lacinato kale, stalks removed, leaves roughly chopped

1 lemon, cut into 4 wedges

Preheat the oven to 425°F. Wash the rice in a few changes of cold water until the water runs clear, then leave to soak in cold water until you're ready to cook it.

Arrange the squash in a single layer on a large sheet pan, drizzle over 3 tablespoons of oil, and season with a pinch of salt and black pepper, then roast for 30 minutes, until tender.

Meanwhile, heat a large lidded saucepan on a medium flame. Put the remaining 2 tablespoons of canola oil into the pan, and add the onions and smoked garlic. Sweat for 8 minutes, then add the spices, chiles, cilantro stems, and 1¾ teaspoons of salt. Cook for 4 minutes, until the onions start to brown, then add the kale.

Drain the rice and gently stir into the pan, then add 2½ cups of warm water. Bring to the boil, put the lid on, then turn the heat down to a whisper and leave to cook for 20 minutes. Take off the heat and leave to steam with the lid still on for a further 10 minutes.

When both the rice and the squash are cooked, gently fold the squash into the rice and tip onto a platter (or spoon onto individual plates). Serve with a generous squeeze of lemon and a scattering of cilantro leaves.

WINTER PILAU with beets, cauliflower, and cilantro chutney

Every Indian auntie has a special pilau recipe that is often the subject of much debate and competitiveness. "I think Asha uses MSG in hers," I once heard one auntie whisper. Now, pilau might sound humdrum, but with some elaboration it becomes an unbridled joy: each grain of rice plump and flavorful; burnished vegetables lying ready to be unearthed; and bright bursts of pomegranate and chile slicing through the comfort blanket. I am now an auntie myself, and I'd be thrilled if my pilau became the topic of conversation in someone else's kitchen.

note / You'll need a blender for this recipe.

Serves 4 as a main /

1⅔ cups basmati rice

1½ lbs cauliflower (½ a big one), broken into bite-size florets

1 lb raw beets, peeled and cut into wedges

¾ lb rutabaga (½ a small one), peeled and cut into ½-inch x 1-inch slices

2½ tsp garam masala

canola oil

salt

1 x 14-oz can of coconut milk

6 cloves of garlic, roughly chopped

¾ inch ginger, peeled

2 green finger (or serrano) chiles

1 tsp ground turmeric

1 medium onion, finely sliced

2½ cups (3½ oz) cilantro, roughly chopped

1 tbsp lemon juice

1 tsp sugar

2 handfuls of pomegranate seeds, to top

Preheat the oven to 425°F. Wash the rice in a few changes of cold water until the water runs clear, then leave to soak in cold water.

Put the cauliflower on a sheet pan in a single layer and put the beets and rutabaga on another sheet pan in a single layer. In a small bowl, mix the garam masala, 5 tablespoons of canola oil, and ¾ teaspoon of salt, then drizzle over the vegetables on both pans and toss to coat. Roast for 25 to 30 minutes, until tender and caramelized in places (the rutabaga and beets may need a little longer).

While the vegetables are cooking, make the sauce for the rice. Put 1¼ cups of the coconut milk into a blender with the garlic, ginger, 1 chile, the turmeric, and ¾ teaspoon of salt, then blitz smooth.

In a large frying pan with a tight-fitting lid, heat 2 tablespoons of oil on a medium heat. Fry the onion for 10 minutes, then add the coconut sauce and cook for 8 minutes, stirring frequently. Add the drained rice with 1⅔ cups of freshly boiled water, and bring to the boil. Put on the lid, turn the heat down to a whisper, and cook for 20 minutes, until the rice is cooked through. Take off the heat, fold through the vegetables, pop the lid back on, and leave to steam for 10 minutes.

While the rice is steaming, make the chutney. Add the remaining ½ cup of coconut milk, the cilantro, the other chile, lemon juice, sugar, and ½ teaspoon of salt. Blend smooth, then scrape into a serving bowl. Transfer the rice to a platter, sprinkle with the pomegranate seeds, and serve with the bowl of chutney alongside.

rice

EGGPLANT LARB with sticky rice and a shallot and peanut salad

V

There is something primally delicious about larb, a salad from Laos in which the dressing is king. Larb is sweet, sour, salty, bitter, and has tons of umami. This recipe is based on one I ate at Supawan in King's Cross, London, one of the finest Thai restaurants I've ever visited.

note / A food processor or spice grinder will make quick work of grinding the peanuts, but you can also crush them with a pestle and mortar.

Serves 4 as a main /

For the rice /
1¾ cups Thai sticky (glutinous) rice

For the larb /
4 small eggplants
canola oil
salt
2 tbsp palm sugar
2 tbsp lime juice
2½ tbsp soy sauce
2 tsp tamarind paste
1½ bird's-eye chiles, very finely chopped

For the salad /
3 tbsp canola oil
2 shallots, halved lengthways and finely sliced
scant ½ tsp salt
5 tbsp peanuts, ground
a large handful of fresh cilantro, finely chopped
40 fresh Thai basil leaves, finely chopped
½ a bird's-eye chile, finely chopped
1 tbsp lime juice

Preheat the oven to 425°F. Put the rice into a sieve and rinse it well under the cold tap, then cover it with cold water and leave to soak for 20 minutes.

In the meantime, cut the eggplants in half lengthways and score a criss-cross pattern on the cut sides. Brush all over with oil and put cut side up on two baking sheets. Bake for 20 minutes, brush the cut side with more oil, and bake for another 20 to 25 minutes, until creamy inside.

Meanwhile, make the rice and the salad. Drain the rice, put it in a lidded saucepan, cover with 2¼ cups of cold water, and add ½ teaspoon of salt. Bring to the boil, then turn down the heat to its lowest setting and simmer for 15 minutes, until all the water has evaporated and the rice is cooked. Cover with the lid, and leave to stand for at least 10 minutes.

To make the salad, heat the oil in a small frying pan on a medium flame and fry the shallots for around 20 minutes, until brown and crisp. Take off the heat and stir in the salt, ground peanuts, herbs, chiles, and lime juice.

To make the larb dressing, put the palm sugar, lime juice, soy sauce, tamarind paste, and chile in a small saucepan with ½ cup of water. Heat, stirring, until the sugar melts, then take off the heat, taste, and add up to ½ teaspoon of salt, if need be.

To serve, put a flat mound of rice on each plate, layer over two eggplant halves, pour on the dressing, and sprinkle the salad on top.

SWEET POTATO AND BROCCOLINI BIBIMBAP

The Korean bibimbap allows for infinite variations. The only hard and fast rule is that the bottom layer should be rice, onto which vegetables, an egg, and plenty of sweet, hot gochujang sauce—a sauce that'll make your taste buds jump for joy—are piled. I like the sweet potato and greens combination in this recipe, but corn, thinly sliced zucchini, roasted cauliflower, leeks, and snow peas also work really well.

Serves 4 as a main /

For the gochujang sauce /

4½ tbsp gochujang paste

3 tbsp toasted sesame oil

1½ tbsp soy sauce

1½ tbsp agave syrup

1½ tbsp rice vinegar

For the vegetables /

2½ tbsp soy sauce

2½ tbsp toasted sesame oil

1 clove of garlic, grated

3 tbsp canola oil

1 lb sweet potatoes (2 medium), peeled and cut into ¼-inch rounds

¾ lb broccolini, big stems cut in half

4 large eggs

2 avocados, pitted, cut into ½-inch slices, and peeled

optional: a handful of mixed seeds (such as pumpkin and sesame), to serve

For the rice /

1¾ cups sushi or short-grain rice

In a small bowl, mix together all the ingredients for the gochujang sauce. Next, in another small bowl, mix together the soy sauce, sesame oil, and garlic for the vegetables and leave to one side.

Place the rice in a medium-sized lidded saucepan and cover with lukewarm water. Stir with your hand until the water turns cloudy. Drain and repeat, until the water runs clear, then cover with warm water and leave to soak for 5 minutes. Drain, then tip the rice back into the saucepan with 1⅔ cups of cold water. Place the pan over a high heat, put the lid on, bring to the boil, then turn the heat down to a whisper and cook for 10 minutes. Take off the heat and leave to steam with the lid on.

For the vegetables, heat 1 tablespoon of oil in a large lidded frying pan. When hot, add the sweet potatoes in a single layer (you may need to fry in two batches). Fry for 3 to 4 minutes on either side (until tender), and place in a bowl to one side. Add another tablespoon of oil to the pan and fry the broccolini. Again, cook in batches if need be. Fry for 2 minutes on each side until the florets are blackening. Then add 2 tablespoons of water to the pan (careful, it may spit), cover, and steam for 3 minutes. Remove the broccolini to the plate with the sweet potatoes, pour over the soy and sesame dressing, and mix.

Finally, add 1 more tablespoon of oil to the frying pan and crack in your eggs. Fry these until the whites are just set and the yolks are still runny.

To build your bibimbap, divide the rice between four bowls. Place a fried egg in the center of each bowl, then put 4 or 5 slices of sweet potato, 5 or 6 stems of broccolini, and 4 slices of avocado around the egg, leaving the yolk and some of the white visible. Drizzle each bowl with a tablespoon of gochujang sauce, sprinkle with seeds (if using), and serve.

PICCALILLI SPICED RICE

Piccalilli is the most strange and wonderful of British condiments. Its neon-yellow presence evokes a world of tea cakes, tennis whites, and summers spent pickling garden vegetables to the sound of cricket on the radio. But it is also a reassuring reminder of the love affair between Britain and India that is still playing out in our kitchens more than 400 years after it started.

The vegetables are best chopped small for this, so be prepared for a reasonable amount of chopping. Fresno chiles, which are often mild, are perfect here, rather than hot bird's-eye chiles.

Serves 4 as a main /

2 lbs cauliflower (1 large)

canola oil

salt

1⅔ cups basmati rice

1½ tsp black mustard seeds

1½ tsp cumin seeds

1 medium red onion, diced

¾ lb carrots (4 medium), peeled and finely diced

3 cloves of garlic, crushed

2 Fresno or other red chiles, finely sliced

½ lb green beans, cut into ¾-inch pieces

4 tsp jarred English mustard

2½ tbsp lemon juice

½ tsp ground turmeric

Preheat the oven to 425°F. Line two sheet pans with foil and cut the cauliflower into bite-size florets no wider than 1 inch. Put in a single layer across the pans, drizzle with oil, and sprinkle with a little salt, then roast for 15 minutes, or until crisp, turning once halfway.

Meanwhile, wash the rice in a few changes of cold water until the water runs clear, then leave to soak in a pan of hand-hot water for 10 minutes. Drain, cover with plenty of freshly boiled water, bring to the boil, and simmer for 10 to 12 minutes, or until tender. Drain again, leave in the sieve over the pan, cover with a clean kitchen towel, and set aside.

Heat 3 tablespoons of oil in a large non-stick frying pan and add the black mustard and cumin seeds. Let them sizzle and pop, then add the onion and carrots. Cook for 10 minutes until both are starting to caramelize, then add the garlic and chiles, and fry for 3 minutes, until the raw smell of garlic disappears. Add the beans, cook for 3 to 4 minutes until tender (but still crunchy), then add the English mustard, lemon juice, turmeric, and 1¾ teaspoons of salt. Stir in the roasted cauliflower, then slowly fold in the rice until everything is well mixed and the rice is a uniform yellow.

Check the rice for mustard, lemon, and salt, and adjust as you wish. Serve with a dollop of yogurt (non-dairy, if vegan) and some mango chutney on the side.

BEET AND YOGURT RICE

VO

In this recipe I married two of my favorite South Indian dishes. The first is curd rice, a dish which has a place in the heart of all Tamilians. It is rice mixed with yogurt and tempered with mustard seeds, curry leaves, and chile. The second is a Keralan beet pachadi, a grated beet dish cooked with garlic, coconut, and cumin seeds. The result is heavenly, flavor-packed, and cooling—a perfect meal for a summer's night.

Serves 4 as a main /

1⅔ cups basmati rice

3 tbsp coconut oil

8 fresh curry leaves

½ tsp cumin seeds

1 tsp black mustard seeds

3 shallots, halved and thinly sliced

3 cloves of garlic, crushed

1–2 green finger (or serrano) chiles (to taste), very finely chopped

¼ cup dried shredded coconut

1 lb raw beets, peeled and grated

1½ tsp salt

1 cup Greek (or thick non-dairy) yogurt

a handful of toasted cashews

Wash the rice in a few changes of cold water until the water runs clear, then drain and leave to soak in cold water for 20 minutes. Tip the drained rice into a medium saucepan, cover with 2 cups of freshly boiled water, and place over a medium heat. Bring to the boil, place the lid on, then turn the heat down to a whisper and cook for 10 minutes. Take off the heat and leave to steam with the lid on while you get on with the rest of the dish.

In a large frying pan for which you have a lid, heat the oil over a medium flame and, when hot—like, really hot (be patient)—add the curry leaves, cumin, and black mustard seeds. Let them crackle and pop, then add the shallots. Cook for 6 minutes until soft and browning, then add the garlic, chiles, and coconut.

Fry the mixture until the coconut is toasted. Remove 2 tablespoons to a bowl to decorate the final dish, then add the beets, salt, and ¼ cup + 1 tbsp of water to the pan. Put the lid on and cook for 10 minutes until the beets are soft, then gently fold in the yogurt. Cook for 2 more minutes, then carefully fold in the cooked rice, in batches, until it is well incorporated. Put the lid back on and allow the dish to rest for 10 minutes.

Sprinkle over the remaining shallot mixture and the toasted cashews, and serve.

HERBED WILD RICE with coconut and lime V

I've always wanted to be the kind of cook who has a flourishing garden, but I haven't quite got there. Instead, I tend to buy large bunches of herbs from my greengrocer, but even with the best intentions they often languish at the bottom of the fridge. When that happens, this recipe is the perfect remedy. It's based on the Malaysian recipe nasi ulam, in which various herbs and toasted coconut are mixed into boiled rice. All you need to do is boil the rice, mix in the other ingredients, and voila, you have a meal: tasty enough to eat by itself or as part of a bigger spread.

note / If you can't find toasted coconut flakes, buy plain ones and toast them for a couple of minutes in a dry pan to bring out the lovely nutty sweetness.

Serves 2 for lunch or 4 as part of a main meal /

1 cup + 1 tbsp wild rice
1 cup basmati rice
1 tbsp salt
½ cup shredded Thai basil leaves
⅓ cup shredded mint leaves
⅓ cup finely chopped cilantro
1 cup fried onions (storebought)
½ cup roasted unsalted peanuts
3 tbsp lime juice (from 2 limes)
3 tbsp canola oil
1 tbsp soy sauce
¼ cup toasted coconut flakes

Wash the rice in a few changes of cold water until the water runs clear, then leave to soak for 20 minutes in cold water. Drain, then place in a lidded saucepan with 6½ cups of freshly boiled water and bring to the boil. Add the salt, and simmer for 20 minutes until the rice is tender. Drain the rice, put it back into the saucepan, cover with the lid, and allow to rest for 10 minutes.

After the rice has rested, allow to cool a little then add all the other ingredients and mix well. Taste and adjust the seasoning if need be, and transfer to a serving platter to serve.

BLACK RICE CONGEE

V

A bowl of congee is China's ultimate comfort food. When your taste buds want something soothing and gentle, congee is the one. There are three elements to congee: the rice, stock, and toppings. I prefer the grains of rice to be intact when cooked, so I've used venere nero rice here, a variety of naturally delicious and nutty rice which doesn't easily break down. I've topped the dish with quick radish pickles. Feel free to have a play around, but some of my favorite toppings include a soy egg (see page 37), fried shallots, chile oil (see page 257), sautéed vegetables, or just a handful of green onions and a drizzle of sesame oil.

Serves 4 as a main /

For the congee /
2 tbsp canola oil

3 cloves of garlic, crushed

½ lb brown mushrooms, roughly chopped

1¼ cups venere nero rice

¼ tsp salt

4¼ cups vegan vegetable stock

1½ tsp soy sauce

For the pickles /
⅓ cup white wine vinegar

2 tbsp sugar

½ cup finely sliced radishes

Place a large saucepan over a medium-high heat and warm the oil. Add the garlic and sweat for a couple of minutes until just browning. Add the mushrooms and cook, stirring regularly, for 10 minutes until dark brown and starting to crisp. Add the rice and salt, and toss and toast in the mushroomy oil for 2 minutes. Pour in the stock and 4¼ cups of water, bring to the boil, reduce the heat to the lowest possible setting, and simmer for 1½ to 1¾ hours, until the rice is falling apart and has no "bite" at all. Take off the heat and stir through the soy sauce.

While the congee is cooking, make the pickle. In a small saucepan over a low flame, combine the vinegar, sugar, and 2½ tablespoons of water, and bring to a simmer so that the sugar dissolves. Place the radishes in a small heatproof bowl and pour over the hot pickling liquor. Put to one side until you are ready to eat the congee. The pickling liquor should turn an exciting pink, and the vegetables will soften slightly.

Serve comforting bowlfuls of the congee with a few pickled radishes on top.

tofu

Few ingredients deserve their own chapter, but tofu definitely does.

Until a couple of years ago, I was a tofu-denier. Like many others, I saw this flavorless bean curd as a substitute for meat and didn't appreciate it as an ingredient in its own right. The dish that changed my mind was chile tofu. I shared a plate with my father at his favorite bolthole, a canteen called Tangoe in Leicester. The tofu was crisp and chewy, giving way to a soft and creamy sponginess, and doused in a sweet, fiery sauce. This is living, I remember thinking—until we got to the last piece. The daughter should surely have it, I thought, but he decided it was the father's right. I am pleased to report that we're still on speaking terms.

TYPES OF TOFU

Firm and extra-firm tofu

These are the types I cook with most frequently at home and use for most of the tofu recipes in this book. They are robust and perfect for pan-frying because they develop a golden crust; but they can also be thrown into soups and stews happily as they are, to absorb the surrounding flavors. The most commonly available type is plain, although I sometimes use smoked. Both can be found in the refrigerated aisles of the supermarket. Plain tofu is sealed in water.

They don't need much in the way of special treatment, but if you're frying them, you'll need to drain the water from the tofu so it doesn't spit in the pan and crisps up nicely. The easiest way to do this is to slide a clean hand underneath the tofu block, like a pizza paddle, and place the other over the top. Over the sink, apply gentle pressure to squeeze out as much water as possible, then place the tofu on some paper towels, swaddle it, and leave for 5 minutes.

To fry it, cut it into pieces, and use a non-stick pan and a little oil. Once in the pan, leave well alone for a few minutes to allow the tofu to brown—this is the key to caramelizing it. Don't panic if it sticks; it should come free once cooked. Sometimes it is worth dredging your tofu pieces in a thin coating of seasoned cornstarch, not only to guarantee crispiness but also so that a sauce properly coats and sticks to it, as with the chile tofu recipe on page 177.

Medium-firm tofu

This is useful to throw into braised dishes or other dishes that don't involve frying (it can fall apart easily when fried), but I tend to stick to firm or extra-firm tofu due to its versatility and the fact that I always have some in the door of the fridge.

Silken tofu

Silken or soft tofu is fragile, creamy, and dairy-like. I love to eat it with a spoon with a crunchy, tart, and tangy dressing over the top (as in my silken tofu with pine nuts and pickled chiles on page 167). It also makes a fantastic spiced scramble (see page 164), which can be served on toast, and is perfect for throwing into a blender to make a sauce or a wonderful vegan mayonnaise (see page 255).

Silken tofu can be bought in shelf-stable cartons or fresh from the fridge. When you're ready to use it, handle it as gently as a baby if you want to keep the block intact. To remove it from the carton in one piece, use a steady hand and a pair of scissors to slice along the carton edges. If you're using it for any other reason, you needn't be quite so cautious. As with the other types of tofu, you'll need to drain the water from it: place the tofu on a plate and leave for 10 minutes or so, then tip the water away before using.

A little note on tempeh

Tempeh isn't technically tofu, but it's Indonesia's own soybean product, made by compressing fermented soybeans together in a block. Like tofu, it doesn't have a strong flavor, but it is earthier, nuttier, and a much heartier ingredient. Some health food shops stock it in the refrigerated section, but you might also find it in a jar. I enjoy it pan-fried with bok choy and tomato sambal (see page 168).

MEDIUM-FIRM TOFU

SMOKED TOFU

TEMPEH

SILKEN TOFU

FIRM TOFU

SCRAMBLED TOFU AKURI

V

Scrambled tofu is not a poor substitute for scrambled eggs but a genuine contender; silken tofu's mild personality makes it a perfect vehicle for louder Indian flavors. Here I've cooked the scrambled tofu akuri-style, which is how the Parsi community eat their scrambled eggs—using the holy trinity of ginger, garlic, and chile, seasoned with cumin and fresh cilantro.

Serves 2 /

1 lb silken tofu

½ tsp cumin seeds

2 tbsp canola oil, plus extra to serve

1 medium red onion, very finely chopped

1 green finger (or serrano) chile, very finely chopped

1 clove of garlic, crushed

½ inch ginger, peeled and grated

1 small ripe tomato, finely chopped

2 tbsp finely chopped cilantro

½ tsp ground turmeric

½ tsp salt

4 slices of bread, toasted, to serve

Line a sieve with paper towels or a clean cloth, carefully place the tofu in the sieve, and allow to drain over a bowl for at least 10 minutes. Place the cumin seeds in a pestle and mortar and crush to a coarse powder.

Heat the oil in a non-stick frying pan and, when hot, add the ground cumin seeds. Stir-fry for a minute until the smell rises, then add the onion. Fry for 8 minutes until soft, sweet, and browning, and add the chile, garlic, and ginger. Fry for 2 minutes, then add the tomato, cilantro, turmeric, and salt.

Take the tofu and crush it between your fingers into the pan (or mash it in the pan with a potato masher). Cook for a few more minutes, until the tofu is piping hot and well mixed with the other ingredients, then serve immediately on toast, drizzled with oil if you wish, alongside ketchup and a pot of chai.

tofu

SILKEN TOFU with pine nuts and pickled chiles

V

Silken tofu is so named because it is passed through silk and is the most delicate of all the tofus both in flavor and texture. This recipe is loosely based on a memorable encounter I had with a silken tofu dish at a restaurant called My Neighbours the Dumplings in east London. The fragility of the tofu contrasted wonderfully with a brute of a dressing: hot and sour with pickled chiles, salty with soy, and crunchy with toasted pine nuts.

note / Buy fresh silken tofu if you can, but if you can only find shelf-stable tofu, make sure you cut carefully along the edges of the carton and open the pack gently so as not to break it up. Pickled chiles can be bought in jars from most supermarkets. Yours may be green, rather than red as in the picture.

Serves 4 as a starter /

14 oz silken tofu

2 tbsp toasted sesame oil

1 tsp white wine vinegar

1½ tbsp soy sauce

½ tbsp agave syrup

½ tbsp canola oil

2 green onions, green part only, finely chopped

⅓ cup pine nuts

2 pickled chile peppers, finely sliced

¼ cup finely sliced cilantro

Remove the tofu from its packaging, put on a plate, and leave for 10 minutes or so, then tip the water away. Place the drained tofu on a nice serving plate with a lip, as things are about to get saucy.

In a medium-sized bowl, combine the sesame oil, vinegar, soy sauce, agave syrup, and 2 tablespoons of hot water. Whisk with a fork to mix.

Put the canola oil into a pan over a high heat and, when hot, add the green onions, pine nuts, and pickled chile peppers. Fry for 2 minutes, stirring every now and then, being very careful not to burn the mixture.

Very carefully (as it may spit), tip the hot pine nuts into the sesame oil mixture along with the cilantro. Mix well, then pour over the tofu and serve.

TEMPEH with bok choy and tomato sambal

V

I wasn't sure I would fall in love with tempeh, but after seeing a particularly tantalizing photo of it looking crisp and delicious in *Fire Islands*, Eleanor Ford's book on Indonesian food, I was emboldened to give it a go. And I'm pleased to report I've found room for it in my heart, particularly in this recipe, where the tempeh is fried to give it crunch then added to tomatoes, garlic, and sweet soy, or kecap manis sauce—with some greens stirred in at the final minute. It's a very satisfying one-pan meal with some rice alongside.

note / Tempeh can be found in health food shops or online. The vacuum-packed stuff is much better than the jarred tempeh. Kecap manis is also available online or from Asian supermarkets—or to make your own, see page 256.

Serves 2 /

14 oz tempeh, each slice cut into
   2 triangles

¼ cup canola oil

4 shallots, very finely chopped

5 fat cloves of garlic, crushed

1 lemongrass stalk base, bottom
   2 inches only, very finely chopped

2 bird's-eye chiles

½ lb ripe tomatoes, chopped

¾ tsp salt

1 tbsp kecap manis

½ lb bok choy, bases cut off and
   shredded lengthways

First, fry the tempeh. Line a plate with paper towels and heat the oil in a non-stick frying pan for which you have a lid. When hot, add the slices of tempeh. Cook for around 2 minutes, until crispy and golden brown, then flip onto the other side and cook for a further 2 minutes. Take off the heat, lever the tempeh out using a spatula (leaving the oil behind), and place on the plate to drain.

Reheat the oil in the same pan over a medium heat and add the shallots. Cook for 8 minutes until browning, then add the garlic, lemongrass, and chiles. Cook for 3 to 4 minutes, until the raw smell of the garlic has gone and the shallots are crispy, then add the tomatoes and stir to mix.

Cook the tomatoes for 8 minutes until you have a delicious soft paste. If it starts to dry out, add a couple of tablespoons of water. Turn the heat right down, stir in the salt and kecap manis, and place the triangles of tempeh back into the pan. Carefully mix again and layer over the shredded bok choy. Turn the heat up, pop the lid on, and cook for 2 minutes.

Take off the heat and transfer to two plates or a serving platter and eat alongside hot rice.

tofu

MUSHROOM MAPO TOFU V

Mapo tofu is a well-loved Sichuanese dish that originated in Chengdu centuries ago. The fact that it is still served in most Sichuan restaurants (and weekly in the Sodha household) gives you some idea of its popularity. My version of this famous dish is made with meaty shiitake mushrooms, leeks, and broth, all layered over with bright Sichuan peppercorns and a magical sauce (toban djan) made of fermented fava beans. The result is flavor amplified—and that never grows old.

note / Many big supermarkets stock Lee Kum Kee chile bean sauce (a fermented fava bean paste). The salted fermented black beans, however, are not so easily found: look online or in Asian supermarkets. If you can't find them, just leave them out and season the dish to taste.

Serves 4 /

1½ tsp Sichuan peppercorns

2 tbsp canola oil

3 cloves of garlic, crushed

½ inch ginger, peeled and grated

½ lb fresh shiitake mushrooms, finely chopped

1 lb leeks (2 small), cut into thin rounds

2 tbsp toasted sesame oil

2 tbsp chile bean sauce

1 tbsp dark soy sauce

2 tsp salted fermented black beans, rinsed and chopped

14 oz firm tofu, drained and cut into ½-inch cubes

2 cups vegan vegetable stock

1½ tbsp cornstarch, mixed with 1½ tbsp water

1 green onion, cut into wispy long strips

Put the Sichuan peppercorns into a mortar and grind well. Take a sniff and revel in their strange and wonderful grapefruit smell.

Heat the canola oil in a large frying pan on a medium flame. Once hot, add the garlic and ginger, and stir-fry for 2 minutes. Add the mushrooms, cook for 6 minutes, then add the leek and stir-fry for a further 2 minutes, until the leeks soften and unravel. Transfer the vegetables to a bowl.

Put the sesame oil, ground Sichuan peppercorns, chile bean sauce, soy sauce, and black beans into the same pan and fry for a couple of minutes, until the oil separates. Add the tofu, stir to coat, then return the vegetables to the pan. Pour over the stock, bring to the boil, then stir in the cornstarch paste and heat until the sauce thickens. Take off the heat and transfer to a serving dish. Garnish with the green onion strips and serve with plain white rice.

CELERY ROOT, TOFU, AND KALE GADO GADO V

Celery root takes the prize as autumn's most flexible root: it can be mashed, grilled, broiled, or eaten raw. Granted, this bulbous, warty fellow won't win awards for looks, and you might need to give its mud-filled crevices a bit of attention, but it's worth it. In this dish, a warm Indonesian salad, I've roasted it, making it charred and crispy, as well as sweet and tender, which perfectly balances the punchy flavors of a classic gado gado dressing, with its peanuts, chiles, and tamarind. Gado gado means "mix mix," which are not bad words to live by in the kitchen (don't get stuck in a rut).

note / I used a seasoned smoked tofu. If yours is unsalted, you might need to sprinkle with a little salt before or after frying.

Serves 4 as a main /

1½ lbs celery root (1 medium), peeled, halved, and cut into ¼-inch slices

1½ lbs fingerling potatoes, quartered

salt

¼ cup canola oil, divided

½ lb curly kale, ribs discarded, leaves roughly torn

1 x 7-oz pack of smoked tofu, cut into ¼-inch-thick slices

For the gado gado dressing /

½ cup + 1 tbsp crunchy peanut butter

2 tsp dark brown sugar

2 tbsp tamarind paste

2 bird's-eye chiles, chopped

1 tbsp soy sauce

½ a clove of garlic, crushed

Preheat the oven to 425°F. Put the celery root, potatoes, a teaspoon of salt, and 2 tablespoons of oil into a roasting pan, toss with your hands to coat everything in oil, then spread out into one flat layer. Roast for 25 minutes, until the celery root and potatoes have burnished edges.

Meanwhile, prepare the kale. In a large bowl, massage a teaspoon of salt and a tablespoon of oil into the kale for a few minutes, until the leaves start to soften, then set aside.

Put all the dressing ingredients into a blender with ⅔ cup of water and pulse until smooth. (You may need a little more water, depending on the thickness of your peanut butter.)

Spread the kale in a single layer on top of the celery root and potatoes, then return the pan to the oven for 8 to 10 minutes, turning the leaves halfway through so they cook evenly (and to ensure they don't burn). The kale is ready when it has started to dry out and is crunchy to the touch. Remove from the oven and leave to one side.

Finally, in a non-stick frying pan over a medium flame, heat the last tablespoon of oil and, when hot, add the tofu and fry for a minute on each side, until golden brown. To assemble the salad, layer the roast celery root and potato with the tofu slices and crunchy kale on a platter, then drizzle over the gado gado dressing and serve.

tofu

HONEY, SOY, AND GINGER BRAISED TOFU

I don't have a restaurant, but if I did, this would be on my "specials" board because it's delicious and I'd want you to try it. This is a rogue version of the Korean braised tofu called dubu jorim. The rogue ingredient is pear, which adds lovely body and a sweetness to the dish. This dish goes well with steamed broccoli and rice.

note / I doubled this recipe when it was photographed, so there is more sauce in the photo than you'll get if you cook one batch (but feel free to double the whole recipe to feed 4 or just the sauce if you like your tofu saucy).

Serves 2 as a main /

10 oz extra-firm tofu

2 tbsp soy sauce

1½ tbsp honey (or agave syrup if vegan)

3 cloves of garlic, crushed

½ inch ginger, peeled and grated

1 Bartlett pear, grated

4 green onions, finely chopped, whites and greens separated

2 tbsp toasted sesame oil

1½ tsp gochujang paste

2 tbsp canola oil

a handful of black and white sesame seeds, to serve

Lightly press the tofu block between your hands over the sink to get rid of as much water as possible, then wrap in paper towels and leave to one side.

Place the soy sauce, honey, garlic, ginger, pear, green onion whites, sesame oil, gochujang, and 1 tablespoon of water into a bowl and whisk to mix. Remove the tofu from the kitchen paper and cut into ½-inch-thick slices.

Coat the bottom of a large non-stick frying pan with the canola oil and line a plate with a couple of sheets of paper towel. Heat the oil until it reaches smoking point and fry the tofu slices for 8 minutes until golden on both sides. Remove the tofu to the plate, allowing the paper to absorb some of the excess oil.

Remove all but a tablespoon of oil from the pan. Add the soy and honey sauce and stir for a minute, then put the tofu back into the pan and cook for 5 minutes until the sauce reduces and becomes glossy and thick.

To serve, place the tofu in a serving dish, pour the sauce over the top, and sprinkle with the sesame seeds and remaining green onion.

tofu

CHILE TOFU

V

Something happens to me when I get within 10 miles of Leicester, a city in central England. I crave chile paneer: I swear I can smell it the closer I get to the city. This Pavlovian response was forged over years traveling with my parents from Lincolnshire to Leicester to shop for spices and saris. At 10 years old, these trips bored me, so my parents regularly employed bribes to keep my sister and me from getting up to no good. Top of the list was a chile paneer washed down with a carton of neon-orange mango juice.

Chile paneer is Indo-Chinese in origin (the first Indo-Chinese restaurant opened in Kolkata just 85 years ago), a fairly new cuisine that has found its way into the hearts and bellies of all Indians. In this vegan version, I've used tofu instead of paneer, fried it until crisp, then doused it in garlic, chiles, tomato, soy, and sugar until sticky, hot, sweet, and sour. There is nothing not to like: it is brazenly addictive stuff.

Serves 4 /

1¾ lbs firm tofu, drained and cut into 1-inch cubes

cornstarch

canola oil

2 tsp cumin seeds, coarsely ground

1 onion, diced

6 cloves of garlic, crushed

1 inch ginger, peeled and grated

4 green finger (or serrano) chiles: 2 very finely chopped, 2 slit down their length

¼ tsp ground black pepper

2 tbsp tomato paste

2 tbsp soy sauce

2 tsp sugar

¾ tsp salt

2 bell peppers (1 red and 1 green, ideally), cut into ½-inch slices

Spread the tofu cubes on a large plate and dust with cornstarch, turning them to coat. Take a deep frying pan with a lid, add enough oil to come ¼ inch up the sides, and heat over a medium flame. Line a plate with paper towels, to place the fried tofu on.

Shake any excess cornstarch off the tofu, then put half the tofu into the hot oil. Fry for 3 minutes, turning regularly with tongs, until golden, then transfer to the paper-lined plate and repeat with the remaining tofu.

Drain all but 2 tablespoons of oil from the pan, then fry the cumin and onion for 10 to 12 minutes, until soft and sweet. Add the garlic, ginger, and chiles, fry for 5 minutes, then add the pepper, tomato paste, soy sauce, sugar, and salt. Stir to mix, cook for 5 minutes, then add the bell pepper strips and ⅓ cup of water. Cover and leave to cook for 8 minutes, stirring every now and then, and adding more water if need be: there should be just enough "sauce" to coat the tofu.

When the peppers are soft, return the tofu to the pan, turn the heat up, and stir to coat the tofu in sauce. Stir-fry for 5 minutes, then take off the heat.

Serve by itself if you're Indian, or with chapattis, greens, or a leafy salad if you're not.

SMOKED TOFU, MUSHROOM, AND ALMOND KHEEMA

V

When it's damp and chilly outside, I turn for warmth to a gaudy, floral notebook of recipes and stories I've collected from my travels in India. One of my husband's favorite dishes is the kheema from the Olympia Coffee House, a Mumbai institution where time goes by as slowly as the ceiling fans. It's a softly spiced, sweet mince, flecked with herbs, and best eaten doused in lime juice with thick slices of white bread. I've created this vegan version to transport us all there, for one meal at least.

note / Smoked tofu comes both seasoned and unseasoned. In the recipe below, I used seasoned, so if yours isn't, you may need to bump up the salt. You'll need a food processor for this recipe.

Serves 4 /

1½ lbs brown mushrooms, roughly chopped

7 oz smoked tofu, chopped

canola oil

1 medium white onion, finely diced

1½ inches ginger, peeled and grated

6 cloves of garlic, crushed

3 green finger (or serrano) chiles, chopped (or to taste)

¾ cup almond flour

1 tsp garam masala

1½ tsp ground cumin

1½ tsp ground coriander

½ tsp ground turmeric

¾ tsp salt

1⅓ cups frozen petite peas, defrosted

½ cup mint leaves, finely chopped

⅓ cup finely chopped cilantro

To serve /

8 rolls or buns

1 medium red onion, very finely chopped

1 lime

optional: mustard oil

Place the mushrooms in a food processor and pulse to a coarse grind, but be careful not to take them too far and turn them into soup. Scrape into a bowl, then blitz the tofu to the same size as the mushrooms and add to the bowl.

Heat 3 tablespoons of oil in a large frying pan over a medium flame and, when hot, fry the white onion, stirring often, for 10 minutes, until translucent and browning. Add the ginger, garlic, and chiles, stir-fry for 2 minutes, then add the almond flour and stir-fry for 4 minutes, until they're a shade darker.

Add the ground spices and salt, mix to combine, then add the mushrooms and tofu, mix again, and leave to cook for 10 to 12 minutes, until the mushrooms have reduced. Finally, stir in the petite peas, cook for 2 minutes, then take off the heat. Pick the mint leaves and finely chop, then stir the finely chopped mint and cilantro through the mushroom-tofu mixture.

Cut the rolls or buns in half and fry them over a high heat in a drizzle of oil until crisp and warm. Serve the kheema alongside the buns on individual plates. Top with the red onion, squeeze over the lime, and finish with a drizzle of mustard oil, if using.

tofu

SPRING VEGETABLE BUN CHA   V

Years ago, when I worked in an office, one of my favorite lunchtime routines was to buy a bun cha noodle salad from a Vietnamese cafe on Theobald's Road in London. Life has moved on and my office is now my home, but when it comes to lunchtime, this is still one of my favorite things to make.

The key to a great bun cha, in my opinion, is the sweet-and-sour nuoc cham dressing, but the herb and peanut garnish also adds a lot to the overall magic, so don't leave that out.

Serves 4 /

3 cups finely shredded red cabbage

canola oil

4 cloves of garlic, cut into paper-thin slices

3 bird's-eye chiles, thinly sliced

⅓ cup soy sauce

3 tbsp lime juice (from 2 limes)

2 tbsp sugar

14 oz extra-firm tofu

salt and ground black pepper

10 green onions, thinly sliced

1⅔ cups peas or mixed peas and fava beans

2½ cups chopped watercress, tough stems discarded

9 oz rice vermicelli noodles

a large handful of salted peanuts, smashed

a handful of fresh cilantro, finely chopped

a handful of fresh mint, finely chopped

Put the cabbage into a medium-sized heatproof bowl. Heat 2 tablespoons of oil in a small saucepan over a low heat and, when hot, add the garlic and chiles. Stir-fry for 2 minutes until the garlic is fragrant, then add the soy sauce, lime juice, sugar, and ½ cup of water. Bring to the boil, take off the heat, and pour over the cabbage.

Lightly press the tofu block between your hands over the sink to extract as much water as possible. Wrap the squeezed tofu in a few sheets of paper towel and press down gently to absorb the excess moisture, then cut into 1-inch cubes. Line a plate with paper towels. Heat 2 tablespoons of oil in a non-stick frying pan on a medium flame, then add the tofu cubes (in batches, if need be) and leave to fry undisturbed for 4 minutes, until a crust forms. Turn the tofu and fry until golden on all sides, adding more oil if need be. Season with salt and pepper, then transfer to the lined plate.

In the same frying pan, heat 2 tablespoons of oil on a high flame, then add the green onions and fry for 6 minutes, until soft. Add the peas, beans (if using), and a scant ½ teaspoon of salt, stir-fry for 2 minutes, then add the watercress. Briefly cook until wilted, then turn off the heat. Cook the noodles according to the package instructions, then drain.

Divide the noodles, tofu, and vegetables between four bowls. Put a little cabbage in each bowl, then ladle as much of its pickling liquid over the top as you would like. Garnish with the smashed peanuts and herbs, then serve.

GRAM
FLOUR

بیسن

500g ℮ 1.1lb

flour
& eggs

When there are flour and eggs, there is always a meal. Because of this, they have become the beating heart of my kitchen—and many others around the world. They are universal ingredients.

But as you travel, the way they are used varies wildly. In the West, in French cuisine, for example, there is the grand tradition of boulangeries and patisseries. Walk down the streets of Paris on any given morning and you will see the locals clutching their daily bread.

In the East, the use of flour and eggs is more varied and subtle, and the curious cook or eater has to look a little harder. I think this is for two reasons. First, in most countries across East and South East Asia the primary crop is rice, not wheat. Second, most homes in the East don't rely on the ovens which we in the West all have in our homes by default. Even in the fast-growing Indian middle classes, the nearest you may find to an oven would be an "OTG"—an oven, toaster, and grill (broiler)—that looks a bit like a microwave and sits on top of the counter asking to be loved but often ignored by the home cook. Instead, the Asian home cook prefers to cook on the stove—meaning the dishes the East more commonly associates with flour and eggs are pancakes and omelets.

Eastern techniques are both familiar and different: a Japanese tamagoyaki (egg tamago roll) is made in a similar way to an omelet, for example, in which eggs are beaten, seasoned (in the case of tamagoyaki, with mirin and soy), and cooked in a pan, the difference in technique being that the egg is cooked in thin layers, rolled up and sliced, ready to be picked up with chopsticks, tucked away into bento boxes, or used to top sushi (see page 202 for my version).

Similarly, the okonomiyaki, a Japanese pancake, is not a world away from an Italian frittata, only the okonomiyaki tends to include a little flour and cabbage and is served drizzled with mayonnaise and okonomiyaki sauce (see page 201).

Vietnam's most famous pancake is made not with wheat and cow's milk but rice flour and coconut milk (see page 197). In Sri Lanka, baked goods, like the seeni sambol bun (see page 188)—a yeasted bun filled with a fiery onion condiment—are a result of British, Portuguese, and Dutch colonization, each wave changing the culinary landscape dish by dish.

Many of the recipes in this chapter are a showcase of what happens when an Eastern flavor meets a familiar Western technique.

A final word on eggs: buy the best you can afford. The best eggs come from the happiest hens with good diets and plenty of room to roam—either pasture-raised hens or those reared on organic farms.

MASHED POTATO PARATHA
with a quick lemon pickle

Beige food has had a difficult few years. We have become so obsessed with what our food looks like that we sometimes forget that what really matters is how it tastes. Aloo (potato) paratha, one of my all-time favorite Indian dishes, will never win a beauty contest, but it is proof that beige can also be brilliant.

note / This recipe is an adapted version of one originally published in the *Guardian*. I've made it easier and quicker by mixing mashed potato and flour together to form a dough, rather than stuffing the dough with potato as is traditional.

Makes 8 /

For the pickle /

2 lemons

2 tbsp canola oil

½ tsp black mustard seeds

1 clove of garlic, thinly sliced

1 Fresno or other red chile, finely chopped

½ tsp salt

For the parathas /

1 lb Russet potatoes, peeled and cut into 1½-inch chunks

2 tbsp canola oil

1 tsp salt

1½ inch ginger, peeled and grated

1½ green finger (or serrano) chiles, very finely chopped

3 tbsp finely chopped fresh cilantro

1 medium red onion, finely diced

½ tsp cumin seeds

1⅔ cups all-purpose flour, plus more for dusting

yogurt, non-dairy if vegan, to serve

First make the pickle. Trim the top and bottom of 1 lemon, cut it into quarters, then, using your sharpest knife, cut each quarter into very thin slices, removing any seeds along the way. Put the slices into a bowl and juice the other lemon over the top. On a very low flame, heat the oil in a lidded frying pan. Add the mustard seeds and garlic, and when the garlic turns pale gold, add the Fresno chile, lemon slices, lemon juice, and ½ teaspoon of salt. Stir, cover, and leave to cook for 5 minutes. Remove the lid, cook for 2 to 3 minutes more, until the oil starts to split from the lemons, then take off the heat and cool.

Bring a pan of water up to a rolling boil. Drop in the potatoes and cook for 12 minutes, or until tender. Drain and, when dry, put back into the same pan. Pour the oil for the parathas into the pan and mash the potatoes really well. Add the salt, ginger, green chiles, cilantro, red onion, and cumin seeds, and mix together. Then add the flour and knead together with your hands until it forms a uniform ball of dough. Lightly flour a surface and lay out a large sheet of parchment paper. Cut the dough ball in half, then cut each half into 4 to make 8 equal pieces. Take a piece and roll it out to a circle about 5½ inches in diameter (dipping the rolling pin in flour where necessary), then transfer to the parchment paper and repeat.

Heat a teaspoon of oil in a shallow non-stick frying pan and, when hot, lay the paratha in. Cook for around 1½ minutes on each side, or until blackened in places and there are no uncooked, doughy spots. As the pan starts to heat up, the parathas will cook more quickly, and you may need to reduce the cooking time or heat. Serve with the lemon pickle and a dollop of cold yogurt.

SEENI SAMBOL BUNS

Seeni sambol is one of Sri Lanka's most delightful offerings: a sweet onion chutney made with cinnamon, cloves, chile, and tamarind. Here it is stuffed into a small pocket of dough enriched with coconut milk, then baked to form a soft, delicious bun.

Makes 8 /

For the seeni sambol /

2 tbsp canola oil

1 lb red onions, finely sliced

2 tsp red chile powder, such as Kashmiri

½ tsp ground cinnamon

¼ tsp ground cloves

1½ tsp tamarind paste

scant 1 tsp salt

For the buns /

1 cup coconut milk, plus 1 tbsp

3 tbsp virgin coconut oil

2 tsp sugar

1 tsp salt

4 cups + 2 tbsp all-purpose flour, plus extra for dusting

2 tsp instant yeast

optional: 1 egg, to glaze

First make the seeni sambol. Put the canola oil into a lidded saucepan over a medium heat. When hot, add the onions, chile powder, cinnamon, cloves, tamarind, and salt and cook for 3 minutes, until the spices smell potent and the onions are softening. Add 2 tablespoons of water and reduce the heat to its lowest, cover with the lid, and cook for 30 minutes, stirring every 10 minutes or so, and adding a few more tablespoons of water if it feels dry. The onions should become a dark, sticky mass. Once cooked, leave to cool.

In a small pan over a low flame, melt together 1 cup of coconut milk, the coconut oil, sugar, and salt. Once the sugar has dissolved, take off the heat and leave to cool.

Put the flour and yeast into a large bowl and mix well. Add 3 tablespoons of lukewarm water and the cooled coconut milk mixture, and bring together into a coarse dough. Dust your work surface with a sprinkle of flour, turn out the dough, and knead for 10 minutes until smooth and springy. Place the dough back in the mixing bowl, cover with a clean kitchen towel, and leave for 30 minutes in a relatively warm place until almost doubled in size. Preheat the oven to 425°F and line a baking sheet with parchment paper.

Tip the dough onto your work surface. Divide into 8 equal pieces, each weighing around 3½ oz. Shape each piece into a rough ball, then press each ball into a flat disk about the size of your palm. Put a heaped tablespoon of seeni sambol into the middle of one disk, bring the sides up and over the filling, and twist to create a sealed bun. Place seam side down on the baking sheet, and repeat with the remaining dough.

Cover the buns again with the clean kitchen towel and leave to proof for 10 minutes in a warm place. If you're using the egg, mix together with the tablespoon of coconut milk and brush each bun with the mixture; if you're not using the egg, just use the coconut milk. Bake in the hot oven for 20 minutes until golden, then leave to cool on a wire rack before devouring.

KIMCHI PANCAKES with a spinach salad   V

When I first discovered kimchi, I nearly ate a whole jar in a single salty, spicy, and sour sitting. A fully formed addict, I went in search of recipes, and became acquainted with the kimchi jeon at Oshibi, a Korean restaurant in York. A jeon is a Korean pancake that forgivingly absorbs tofu and most vegetables you might throw at it, but still (quite considerately) becomes crisp, given enough time in the pan. The dipping sauce doubles up as the salad dressing in this recipe, making the salad perfect to throw on top of the pancakes.

Serves 2 as a main or 4 as part of a larger meal /

1 heaping cup chopped kimchi (suitable for vegans)

⅔ cup rice flour

⅔ cup all-purpose flour

1 tsp salt

7 oz firm tofu, drained and cut into thin slivers

a big handful of mung bean sprouts

5 green onions, trimmed and finely chopped

4 packed cups baby-leaf spinach

canola oil

For the dipping sauce /

3 tbsp dark soy sauce

2 tbsp toasted sesame oil

1½ tbsp rice vinegar

2 tsp chile flakes

1 tsp toasted sesame seeds, plus extra to garnish

Tip the kimchi into a sieve over a liquid measuring cup, and press down to extract as much juice as possible. Measure the juice and, if need be, top it up to just under 1 cup with tap water. Roughly chop the drained kimchi.

In a large bowl, use a fork to whisk the flours and salt, then stir in the kimchi juice. Add the kimchi, tofu, bean sprouts, and most of the green onions—save a small handful of the onions for the sauce—and stir again. The batter should be wet but scoopable. Leave to stand for 10 minutes.

Meanwhile, make the dipping sauce. In a small bowl, mix the soy sauce, sesame oil, vinegar, chile flakes, the reserved green onions, and the sesame seeds. Shred the spinach and put into a salad bowl. Add 2 tablespoons of dipping sauce and toss to coat.

To cook the pancakes, heat ½ tablespoon of oil in a medium frying pan (ideally non-stick) on a medium flame and swirl it around to coat the base of the pan. Pour in a quarter of the batter and spread it out with the back of a spoon until it's 6 inches in diameter. Cook for 3 to 5 minutes, until the bottom is crisp and golden, then flip and cook on the other side until that, too, is crisp and golden. Transfer to a warm plate, cover with foil, and repeat with the remaining batter, adding a little extra oil to the pan for each pancake, if need be.

Serve warm with a big handful of spinach salad scattered on top and sprinkled with sesame seeds. Serve the sauce in little bowls on the side.

SODHA FAMILY MASALA OMELET

Every Sunday, Mum used to make us kids a masala omelet each, served with toast and chai in a much-treasured flowery Royal Doulton teapot. But since acquiring husbands, children, and dogs, we've needed a bigger omelet. This masala omelet is similar to the original, but made in much the same way as a frittata: in a single pan and with more eggs, finished off under the broiler.

note / You'll need a non-stick frying pan that can go under a broiler. A 10-inch-diameter pan is perfect.

Serves 4 /

1 tbsp canola oil

2 tbsp unsalted butter

1 medium red onion, finely chopped

1–2 green finger (or serrano) chiles (to taste), very finely chopped

2 cloves of garlic, crushed

⅔ tsp salt

½ lb brown mushrooms, chopped

8 large eggs

½ cup finely sliced cilantro

Heat the oil and butter in a pan over a medium heat. When hot and foaming, add the onion, chiles, garlic, and salt. Cook for 6 minutes, until the onion is translucent and the garlic fragrant, then add the mushrooms. Spread the mushrooms out in one layer to allow them to get crispy. You want the water to evaporate and the mushrooms to start to brown, which should take around 12 minutes.

Meanwhile, switch the broiler on to the maximum setting. Crack the eggs into a bowl, beat well with a fork, mix in the cilantro, and leave to one side.

When the mushrooms are brown, pour in the egg and cilantro mixture. Mix quickly with a wooden spoon, then shake the pan to even the mixture out, and cook for 2 minutes. Take the pan off the stove and carefully pop it under the broiler (with the handle sticking out toward you). Cook for 2 to 3 minutes or until starting to brown on top, then take out and place on a heatproof surface. Slide a spatula around the outside and slide onto a big plate.

Serve with hot buttered toast for breakfast, or with a lemon-dressed salad for a light lunch.

TOMATO, PISTACHIO, AND SAFFRON TART

I believe in low-effort, high-reward cooking, especially when the weather is good and I don't want to be in the kitchen. That's when we all need shortcuts, and this tart is a good example. There's not much to the making of it: the pastry is frozen, the nuts and coconut milk form a base at the push of a button, leaving you just the short task of frying some onions, layering the tomatoes, and popping it in the oven before eating. It's very rich, so you won't need much alongside. Buy full-fat coconut milk, don't shake the can, and leave it to settle so you can scrape the thick cream from the top.

note / Pepperidge Farm frozen puff pastry is suitable for vegans. It is available in 9-inch x 9-inch square sheets, so you will make two square tarts, instead of the rectangle pictured. You'll need a food processor.

Serves 4 /

canola oil

2 medium red onions, halved and thinly sliced

2 tsp tamarind paste

salt

⅔ cup raw pistachio kernels

½ cup almond flour

3 cloves of garlic, roughly chopped

1½ tsp ground cumin

1½ tsp ground coriander

¾ tsp ground cinnamon

a big pinch of saffron

1 cup top of canned coconut milk

2 x 8½-oz puff pastry sheets, defrosted

1½ lbs mixed ripe small red and yellow tomatoes, halved or sliced

Preheat the oven to 475°F. Put 3 tablespoons of oil into a large frying pan on a medium flame and, once hot, add the onions and cook for up to 15 minutes, stirring occasionally, until soft, caramelized, and sweet. Stir in the tamarind paste and ¼ teaspoon of salt, then scrape into a bowl.

Put the nuts, almond flour, garlic, spices, saffron, and ¾ teaspoon of salt into the bowl of a food processor. Open the coconut milk, scrape the cup of cream at the top into the bowl, then process to a smooth paste.

To build the tart, line one or two baking sheets with parchment paper and lay the pastry sheets on top. With a small knife, score a line all around each pastry sheet ½ inch away from the edge. Using a knife or the back of a large spoon, spread the pistachio paste evenly over both sheets, up to the border, then carefully spread the onion mix over the paste. Lay the tomato pieces on top (cut side up if they're in halves)—make sure they're very close to each other, because they will shrink when they cook—then drizzle with oil and sprinkle with a little salt.

Bake for 10–15 minutes, or until the tomatoes are blistered and caramelized and the pastry's edges have puffed up.

VIETNAMESE COCONUT PANCAKES

The Vietnamese really are masters of the mouthwatering salad. They can take raw vegetables and elevate them to heavenly places using a secret weapon, nuoc cham chay—a bright, hot, sweet, and sour sauce that will wake up every neuron in your brain. Here the salad and its dressing are tucked away in a deliciously crispy coconut and turmeric pancake.

Makes 6 pancakes /

1¾ cups rice flour

¾ tsp salt

½ tsp ground turmeric

1 large egg

1¾ cups coconut milk

3 cups finely shredded red cabbage

⅓ lb carrots (2 medium), julienned

5 green onions, finely chopped

1 cup roughly chopped fresh mixed
  herbs (Thai basil, cilantro, and mint)

¼ cup + 1 tbsp lime juice

3½ tsp sugar

1½ tbsp soy sauce

1½ bird's-eye chiles, finely chopped

2 cloves of garlic, crushed

canola oil

First make the batter for the pancakes. Put the rice flour, salt, turmeric, and egg into a bowl and mix together. Add the coconut milk and ¾ cup of water, whisk until you have a smooth batter, then leave to one side.

Next, place the cabbage, carrots, green onions, and herbs into another bowl and mix with your hands. Make the sauce by putting the lime juice, sugar, soy sauce, chiles, and garlic into a measuring cup or small bowl and mixing well. Pour two-thirds of this sauce over the vegetables and mix again using your hands. Pour the remaining third into a little serving bowl.

To make the pancakes, heat a teaspoon of oil in a large non-stick frying pan over a medium flame, and swirl it around the pan to coat. When the pan is very hot, pour in a ladleful of batter, swirling the pan quickly and carefully so that the batter reaches the edge. Cook for 2 to 3 minutes until golden and crisp on the bottom (test this by sliding an offset spatula under the pancake; if it lifts away easily, it's ready). Slide onto a plate and repeat with the rest of the batter, until you have 6 pancakes in total. As with all pancakes, your first one might not be perfect, but don't lose faith, you will quickly get the hang of it.

To serve, place a small handful of the salad in the middle of the pancake and roll up. Serve with the extra sauce on the side.

SUN HOUSE CHILE EGGS

Geoffrey Dobbs is a rare breed of man. He throws great parties, he runs a renowned literary festival, he recommends books he thinks you might like. He listens, he challenges, he broadens your horizons. He's the friend everyone should have. He owns the hotel the Sun House in Galle, Sri Lanka—that's where he serves these chile eggs. Like Geoffrey, they are simply brilliant.

Serves 2 /

2 tbsp unsalted butter

1 small red onion, very finely chopped

1–1½ green finger (or serrano) chiles (to taste), very finely chopped

2 cloves of garlic, crushed

½ lb ripe tomatoes, finely chopped

½ tsp salt

4 large eggs

½ cup grated sharp cheddar cheese

a little fresh cilantro, roughly chopped

Put the butter into a large non-stick frying pan over a medium heat and, when it starts to foam, add the onion, chiles, and garlic. Fry for 5 minutes until the onion softens, then add the tomatoes and salt. Fry for another 5 minutes until the tomatoes start to soften, then make four holes in the mixture using a spatula.

Gently crack the eggs into the four holes and leave to fry. When they are almost ready (i.e., the whites near the yolks are nearly set), sprinkle the cheese around the eggs, avoiding the yolks. Fry until the whites at the top of the eggs are set but the yolks still runny, sprinkle with cilantro, and serve immediately.

NAPA CABBAGE OKONOMIYAKI

Okonomiyaki is a type of savory Japanese pancake, and it means "cooked as you like it"—which in my case means laden with lots of sauce, crispy fried onions, and a smattering of fresh green onions.

note / An 8-inch non-stick frying pan is perfect for this pancake.

Makes 2 pancakes (to serve 2) /

For the okonomiyaki /
1¼ cups all-purpose flour
1¼ tsp salt
4 large eggs
4 cups shredded Napa cabbage
6 green onions, finely chopped, whites and greens separated
2 tbsp canola oil

For the okonomiyaki sauce /
2½ tbsp ketchup
2½ tbsp A1 sauce
2½ tbsp date syrup

To serve /
mayonnaise
crispy fried onions (storebought)

Whisk the flour, salt, eggs, and ⅔ cup of water together with a fork in a mixing bowl until there are no lumps and you have a smooth batter. Add the cabbage and the green onion whites, and mix well to coat all the vegetables. Now make the okonomiyaki sauce: put the ketchup, A1 sauce and date syrup into a small bowl and mix well.

To cook the okonomiyaki, heat a tablespoon of oil in a small frying pan over a medium-high flame. Add half the batter to the pan and flatten it with a spoon or spatula to help it into a circular pancake around 1 inch deep. Cook the first side for 3 to 4 minutes. You should see the scraps of cabbage and batter at the edges of the pancake starting to brown and crisp. If it is browning too fast, turn down the heat a little. When it's ready, turn the okonomiyaki with a spatula (or, if you are particularly confident, toss it like a pancake) and cook on the other side for a further 3 minutes. Turn out onto a plate, and repeat with the second half of the batter.

To serve, criss-cross the surface of the okonomiyaki with the sauce and some mayonnaise, then liberally top with crispy onions and the reserved green onions.

EGG TAMAGO ROLLS with wasabi mayo

These egg rolls are made in much the same way as an omelet (here seasoned with mirin and soy), which is then rolled and sliced into bite-size pieces. I eat them for breakfast, snacks, at my desk, and on picnics. In short, there's no occasion I can think of which is not made tastier by the addition of an egg tamago roll.

Serves 2 /

For the wasabi mayo /
¾ tbsp wasabi paste
3 tbsp mayonnaise
1 tsp white wine vinegar
a few black sesame seeds,
    to decorate

For the tamago roll /
4 large eggs
1 tbsp soy sauce
1 tbsp mirin
¾ tbsp black sesame seeds
a pinch of salt
canola oil
2 sheets of nori

First make the wasabi mayo. In a small bowl, combine the wasabi, mayo, and vinegar. Stir to mix, sprinkle over a few black sesame seeds, and leave to one side.

To make the tamago batter, break the eggs into a bowl and add the soy sauce, mirin, black sesame seeds, and salt. Beat well with a fork until well mixed.

Put 1 teaspoon of oil into a non-stick frying pan over a medium heat and swirl to coat the bottom of the pan. When hot, add half the egg mixture. Swirl to coat the bottom of the pan and cook for 1 minute, then place a nori sheet flat on top of the egg. Let it set for a few seconds and then, with a spatula, gently start to roll the egg from right to left. When you reach the end, slide out onto a plate and repeat.

Slice the egg rolls into ¾-inch-wide spirals and dunk freely into the mayonnaise.

BOMBAY ROLLS

Standing three tiers high, the magnificent Bombay sandwich is a whopper of a construction. It's available on every street corner, and each stallholder obsesses over their own special blend of spices, vegetables, and chutneys, for that "better than yours" taste. Although it's a wonder, it's also a labor of love to make at home, and so in this recipe I've attempted to embody its spirit—a sharp, hot green chutney, cheese, and onion—but in a pastry roll that can be made in just minutes.

Makes 8 /

1½ cups roughly chopped cilantro

½ cup roughly chopped mint leaves

2 tsp lemon juice

2 green finger (or serrano) chiles, roughly chopped

1 tsp ground cumin

1¼ tsp salt

2 tbsp canola oil

all-purpose flour, to dust

1 x 14-oz puff pastry sheet, defrosted

1 cup extra sharp cheddar cheese, grated

½ a small red onion, very finely sliced

1 egg, beaten with a pinch of salt

Preheat the oven to 425°F and line a 9-inch x 16-inch baking sheet with parchment paper.

Put the cilantro, mint, lemon juice, chiles, cumin, salt, and oil into a blender, and pulse until you have a smooth chutney that is thick and spreadable. Taste: it should be hot, herby, salty, and sour all at once. If it isn't, adjust as you see fit.

Sprinkle a little flour over your work surface and lay out the pastry. Spread the surface of the pastry with the cilantro chutney, leaving a 1-inch strip free along the top edge (the side farthest from you). Add the cheddar in a similarly even layer and scatter the onion over the top, then brush the exposed strip with beaten egg.

Roll the pastry in a tight spiral away from you until you have a big jelly roll. Cut the roll into 1½-inch-wide pieces and lay each piece on the baking sheet with a 2-inch gap between them. Brush each cut side with egg, then place in the hot oven and cook for 20–25 minutes or until the tops are golden brown and caramelized. Allow to cool slightly before separating and eating.

See photos overleaf

BOMBAY ROLLS

LEEK AND CHARD MARTABAK

Depending where in the world you are, martabak are stuffed breads, pancakes, or small pastries, thought to have originated from the Indian community in Yemen and spread through the Indian trading routes in the Middle East and Asia. Now they are sold by street vendors from Saudi Arabia to Singapore and Indonesia to Malaysia. Here, I've omitted the usual ground meat and used chard, leeks, and onions instead, all bound together with egg and the quite untraditional (but very delicious) cheese.

Serves 8 /

canola oil

2 medium red onions, finely chopped

2 medium leeks, thinly sliced

6 green onions, finely sliced

4 cloves of garlic, crushed

¾ inch ginger, peeled and grated

1 lb chard, stems chopped into ½-inch pieces, leaves shredded

1 tsp salt

2 tsp ground cumin

2 tsp ground coriander

4 large eggs

2¼ cups sharp cheddar cheese, grated

6 phyllo sheets, defrosted

Preheat the oven to 400°F.

Heat 2 tablespoons of oil in a large lidded frying pan over a medium flame. When hot, add the red onions, leeks, and green onions and cook for 10 minutes, stirring occasionally, until the whole mixture is soft and starting to brown nicely. Add the garlic, ginger, and chard stems and cook for 5 minutes, then add the salt, spices, and chard leaves, mix, and place the lid on the pan. Turn the heat down low and allow the chard to steam in the pan for 5 minutes. Take off the heat, remove the lid, and allow to cool to room temperature.

Place the eggs and cheese in a mixing bowl and beat with a fork. Next, brush a 9½-inch x 13-inch pan with oil. Lay 2 sheets of phyllo across the width of the pan, overlapping them slightly in the center and allowing them to hang out of the pan at the sides. Brush these sheets with a little more oil. Lay 2 more sheets lengthways in the pan, also making sure they hang over the ends of the pan, and brush them with oil.

Add your cooled vegetable mixture to the cheese and eggs, stirring to combine. Empty the filling into the center of the baking pan and use the back of a spoon to level it, making sure the filling reaches each corner of the pan. Take the overhanging phyllo sheets and lay them over the top of the filling, as if you were wrapping a present (don't worry if they don't meet in the middle). Brush those sheets with oil, then lay another sheet lengthways over the top, brush with oil, and then lay the final sheet. Brush the top of the martabak with oil, and trim off any excess pastry around the edge. Place in the hot oven for 25 minutes, until golden brown, and brittle to the touch. Allow to cool, then cut into squares and serve.

KOREAN EGG BREAD

Korean egg bread, or gyeran-bbang, is a popular winter street-food snack in South Korea, but it's also an incredibly addictive loaf to have lying around the kitchen for breakfast, lunch, and all the times in between. In Korea, the bread is flavored with a variety of things, from mozzarella to mayonnaise, and the eggs are cracked whole into the batter. Here I've used smoky paprika and parsley to flavor the bread and soft-boiled the eggs—meaning that you get an excellent egg cross-section when the loaf is sliced.

note / You'll need a deep 10-inch x 5-inch loaf pan for this recipe. If you can't obtain self-rising flour, add 1 tablespoon baking powder and ½ teaspoon salt to 2 cups of all-purpose flour.

Serves 8 /

5 large eggs

2 cups self-rising flour

Heaping ½ cup sharp cheddar cheese, grated

1¼ tsp salt

1½ tsp baking powder

1 tsp hot smoked paprika

½ tsp chile flakes

½ cup finely chopped Italian parsley leaves

7 tbsp unsalted butter, melted, at room temperature

1 cup whole milk, at room temperature

Preheat the oven to 400°F and line your loaf pan with parchment paper.

Bring a small pan of water to a rolling boil and gently lower in 3 eggs using a tablespoon. Cook them for exactly 7 minutes, then drain and remove the eggs, cool the saucepan down under the tap, and fill with very cold water. Pop the eggs in to cool down until needed.

Put the flour, cheddar, salt, baking powder, paprika, chile flakes, and parsley into a large bowl and mix well. Put the melted butter and milk into another bowl, beat the remaining 2 eggs in a separate bowl, then add them to the butter and milk. Add the milk mixture to the flour, mixing it in well until smooth, then pour half the batter into the loaf pan.

Peel the boiled eggs and take a thin slice off the top and bottom of each egg (this helps them to sit next to each other in the batter). Place the eggs in a line along the length of the pan, then slowly and gently push them down into the batter. Spread the rest of the batter over the eggs so they are completely covered.

Put the pan into the center of the hot oven and cook for 55 minutes, or until a skewer inserted into the cake comes out clean. Remove from the oven, leave to rest in the loaf pan for 5 minutes, then turn out onto a wire rack and leave to cool. To serve, eat warm spread with butter, or cold just by itself.

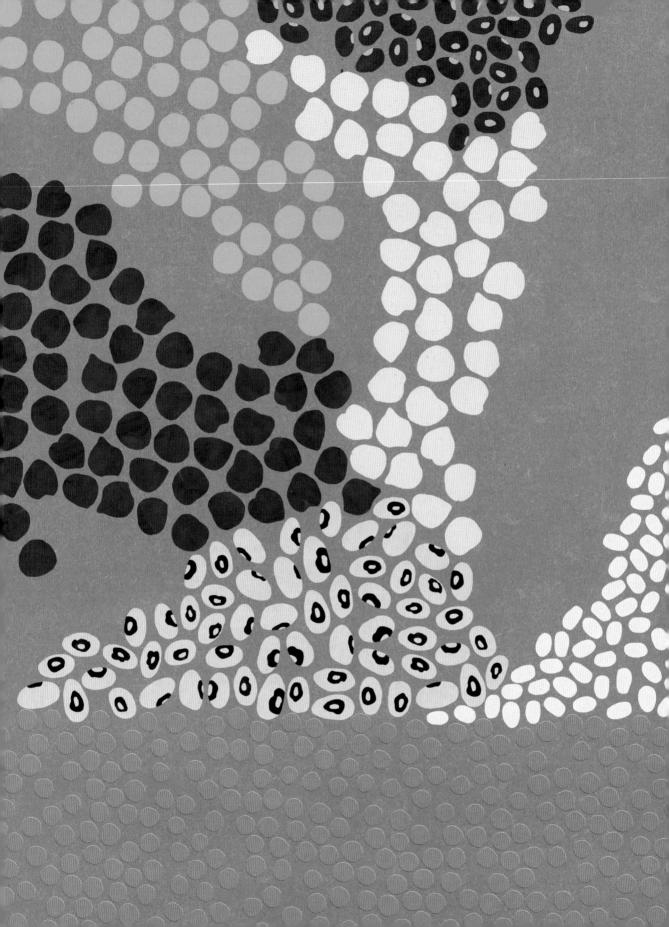

legumes

Lentils, chickpeas, and beans taste of comfort to me.

As a family, we Sodhas ate dal week in, week out, and despite leaving home a couple of decades ago I have never tired of it and still cook dal for my own family at least once a week.

I confess the dal recipes that I lean toward these days use either quick-cooking lentils, like mung dal (the yellow split insides of the mung bean) or red lentils—which both cook in under 30 minutes and don't need soaking. I am also a fan of canned chickpeas, which I simmer so that they lose their chalkiness and become plump and soft: this is so I can spend less time in the kitchen and more at the table. Recipes where the cooking is slow but the preparation is quick also work for me—such as my black dal (see page 215), which you can leave on the stovetop to cook, stirring when you pass.

One of the biggest discoveries in researching legumes for this book was how prevalent and diverse the use of legumes is in India and just how difficult it was to find savory legume dishes from China, Japan, and Korea. According to the UN Food and Agriculture Organization, this is because in these countries legumes are still regarded as "exotic." Their farming traditions revolve around wheat, rice, "and a single [legume], the soybean, whose prominence in the region has been immense."

This fills me with excitement at what a new world of legume dishes from these countries could look like in the future. However, as we are not yet at that point, the recipes in this chapter revolve around the countries in which they are part of everyday life: India, Sri Lanka, Pakistan, and Burma.

QUICK COCONUT DAL
with tomato sambol

V

This dal is a friend in the kitchen. I wrote the recipe just after having my daughter, when I was still a little broken and exhausted. It needs only 5 minutes' or so hands-on work before heat, time, and the ingredients take care of the rest. The dal soothes while the sambol revives.

Serves 2 /

For the dal /

2 tbsp canola oil

1 medium red onion, finely chopped

10 fresh curry leaves, plus extra to serve

2 cloves of garlic, crushed

1 green finger (or serrano) chile, very finely chopped

1 lemongrass stick, cut in half on an angle

1 cinnamon stick, broken in half

¾ cup + 1 tbsp red lentils

⅓ tsp ground turmeric

1 x 14-oz can of coconut milk

1¼ tsp salt

½ tbsp lime (from ½ a lime)

For the tomato sambol /

⅓ cup dried shredded coconut

1 Fresno or other red chile, very finely chopped

¼ lb cherry tomatoes, chopped

1 tbsp lime juice (from 1 lime)

½ tsp salt

Warm a tablespoon of oil in a medium-sized saucepan over a medium heat and add three-quarters of the onion (reserve the rest for the sambol), the curry leaves, garlic, chile, lemongrass, and cinnamon stick. Fry for 5 minutes, then stir in the lentils and turmeric. Add the coconut milk and 1¾ cups of water (fill up the empty coconut can to measure this) and tip it into the pan. Bring the mixture to the boil and simmer for around 20 to 25 minutes, until the lentils are no longer chalky and are tender to the bite. Add more water if it's too thick, then season with the salt and lime.

While the dal is cooking, make the sambol. Place the dried shredded coconut into a heatproof bowl. Pour in 3 tablespoons of freshly boiled water and stir to mix. Add the reserved onion, chile, tomatoes, lime, and salt. Mix, taste, and add more salt to balance if need be.

To serve, fish the cinnamon and lemongrass pieces out of the dal, if you wish, and transfer to a serving bowl. Warm the final tablespoon of oil in a pan over a high heat, and when very hot add a handful of curry leaves and wait for them to crisp up, then take off the heat. Place the sambol over the top or serve on the side and tip the curry leaves over the top of the dal. Serve with rice or paratha.

BLACK DAL V

This is a vegan adaptation of my dairy-rich dal makhani (makhani means "with butter" in Hindi). Despite this omission, it has a wonderful richness to it because the beans release a dense liquid as they cook, which binds the flavors together and gives it a gorgeous thickness. After some initial effort you can largely leave this dal to its own devices, as the longer it cooks the better.

note / You'll need to soak the beans for at least 6 hours before cooking.

Serves 4 /

1½ cups whole black gram (urad beans)

3 tablespoons canola oil

1 cinnamon stick

1 bay leaf

2 medium red onions, chopped

1 inch ginger, peeled and grated

6 large cloves of garlic, crushed

1 x 14-oz can of petite diced tomatoes

2 tbsp tomato paste

1½ tsp salt

1 tsp ground cumin

1 tsp ground coriander

¼ tsp ground turmeric

¾ tsp red chile powder, such as Kashmiri

½ tsp garam masala

optional: 1 tsp kasuri methi (see the note on page 115)

In a sieve, rinse the black gram in cold water until the water runs clear, then drain and put into a deep pan—the beans will double in volume while soaking. Cover with a generous amount of just-boiled water and leave to soak for anywhere between 6 and 24 hours.

Drain the soaked beans, put them back into the pan, and cover with cold water. Bring to the boil, scraping off any scum that appears on top, then cook until tender—this will depend on your beans (older beans take longer to cook), so start checking after 20 minutes. Once boiled, the beans should be soft enough to crush against the side of the pan. Take off the heat and drain some of the liquid off, keeping just enough to cover the beans.

Meanwhile, put the oil into a large frying pan over a medium heat. When hot, add the cinnamon stick, bay leaf, and onions and fry for 15 minutes, then add the ginger and garlic and fry for another 5 minutes. Stir in the canned tomatoes and tomato paste, then leave to simmer for around 12 minutes, until the tomatoes have reduced and are starting to release oil back into the pan. Now stir in the salt and spices, including the kasuri methi, if using. Cook for a couple of minutes, then add to the pot of beans. Bring to the boil, then turn the heat down to a simmer.

Stir every now and then for around 1 to 1½ hours, and when the dal looks too thick or starts to dry out, top it up with some more freshly boiled water and mix. After around an hour, the dal will start to turn dark and the beans and the tomatoes will come together into one silky rich mass. If this doesn't happen, give it some more time—you can't do this dish any harm by cooking it for a little longer.

Taste, adjust the salt and chile if necessary. Serve alongside parathas or hot fluffy naan bread.

BUNNY CHOW

V

I'm well aware that Durban, where bunny chow hails from, is in South Africa, not Asia. But given that Durban is home to more Indians than any other city outside India, I hope you'll forgive me. Indians have been leaving the motherland for years, but they never quite give up their food culture. This has led to some legendary creations, one of which is this hollowed-out loaf, traditionally filled with a bean curry. It's now one of South Africa's most popular dishes and deserves to migrate once more, from Durban to wherever your kitchen table happens to be.

note / You will come across cans of black chickpeas in Indian supermarkets—they are nutty, musky, and often in salted water, so season them discriminatingly. If you can't find them, normal chickpeas will work just as well.

Serves 4 as a main /

4 large rolls or unsplit buns

3 tbsp canola oil

1 medium onion, finely diced

1½ green finger (or serrano) chiles, very finely chopped

3 cloves of garlic, crushed

1½ lbs green cabbage, finely shredded

1 tsp ground cumin

½ tsp garam masala

1 tsp ground turmeric

1¼ tsp salt

1 x 14-oz can of black chickpeas, drained

½ lb snow peas

6 cups (½ lb) baby-leaf spinach

½ cup finely chopped cilantro

1 lemon, cut into 8 wedges

Preheat the oven to 400°F. Cut off the top from each roll and scoop out the bread inside (pop this in a freezer bag and freeze for the next time you need to make breadcrumbs). Put the hollowed-out rolls to one side.

In a wide frying pan with a lid, heat the oil on a medium flame, then stir-fry the onion and chiles for about 6 minutes, until soft and translucent. Add the garlic and fry, stirring, for another couple of minutes. Stir in the cabbage and ¼ cup of water, pop on the lid, and leave to cook for about 8 minutes, until the cabbage is soft and wilted. Stir in the cumin, garam masala, turmeric, and salt. At this point, put the rolls and their lids into the oven and set a timer for 8 minutes.

Add the chickpeas and snow peas to the cabbage pan, stir, and leave to cook for a couple of minutes, then add the spinach handful by handful. Cover the pan again and leave to cook for about 5 minutes, until the spinach has properly wilted, then gently stir through the cilantro.

Take the rolls out of the oven and scoop the vegetable mixture into the cavities. Top with the lids and serve with lemon wedges to squeeze over. Encourage everyone to tear off the bread in big chunks and dip them into the curry filling.

BLACK-EYED PEA AND CHICKPEA USAL   V

Despite the UK being a nation of curry lovers, for the most part, Indian restaurants have been serving us the same old things since the 1940s. That was when the gentlemen from Sylhet in Bangladesh, most of whom came to the UK on boats with the returning British at the end of the British Raj, embarked on a plan to serve curry on our high streets. This recipe for usal, a mixture of legumes and peas in a light, spiced tomato broth, is one I'd love to see more UK restaurants adopt.

note / You can swap the beans and legumes listed for whatever you have to hand: I particularly like sprouted mung beans in my usal, but they're not easy to find in stores and take a few days to sprout from scratch. This is best eaten with a hunk of bread for mopping up the spicy juices.

Serves 4 /

¼ cup canola oil

2 medium red onions, chopped

2 green finger (or serrano) chiles, very finely chopped

4 cloves of garlic, crushed

½ lb ripe tomatoes, chopped

1¾ tsp salt

1 tsp red chile powder, such as Kashmiri

1 tsp garam masala

1 tsp ground cumin

½ tsp ground turmeric

1 x 14-oz can of black-eyed peas, drained

1⅔ cups frozen petite peas, defrosted

1 x 14-oz can of chickpeas, drained

½ lb snow peas

1 tbsp lemon juice

a handful of fresh cilantro leaves, finely chopped

Heat the oil in a pot over a high flame. When hot, add the onions and chiles and cook for 10 minutes, stirring frequently, until the onions look like pink jewels. Stir in the garlic, cook for 2 minutes, then add the tomatoes. When the tomatoes have broken down and become paste-like (around 5 minutes), add the salt and spices, and stir-fry for a minute.

Pour 1 quart of water into the pot, bring it to a boil, then turn down the heat to medium and leave to bubble away for 8 minutes. Stir in the black-eyed peas, petite peas, chickpeas, and snow peas, cook for about 5 minutes, then take off the heat.

Mix in the lemon juice and cilantro, taste, and adjust the seasoning if need be. Divide the peas and legumes between four bowls, ladle the spiced broth on top, and serve.

RED LENTIL RASAM with roasted red cabbage   V

There are dals to comfort and dals to revive. Rasam is a reviver, the kind of thing I want to eat when I'm feeling sluggish. It's thinner than your average dal, brothy and buzzing with spices, with a defined, sour edge. Here, I've served it with my current addiction, roasted red cabbage, whose leaves sweeten, soften, and char in the heat of the oven.

Serves 4 /

1 red cabbage, quartered

canola oil

salt

2 tbsp tamarind paste, divided

1½ tsp cumin seeds

1½ tsp coriander seeds

10 fresh curry leaves

1½ tsp mustard seeds

1 tsp red chile powder, such as Kashmiri

½ tsp ground black pepper

5 cloves of garlic, crushed

1 x 14-oz can of petite diced tomatoes

1⅓ cups red lentils

Preheat the oven to 400°F. Put the quartered cabbage on a lined roasting pan, drizzle with oil, sprinkle with a pinch or two of salt, and roast for 35 minutes.

While the cabbage is cooking, make a tamarind dressing. In a small bowl, mix 2 teaspoons of tamarind paste, 2 teaspoons of water, and a teaspoon of oil. After 25 minutes, when the cabbage is tender to the core and starting to crisp and burn at the edges, remove and brush its cut sides generously with the mixture of tamarind. Return to the oven for 10 minutes, then set aside.

To make the rasam, coarsely grind the cumin and coriander seeds with a pestle and mortar. Heat 2 tablespoons of oil in a large saucepan over a medium heat and, when hot, add the curry leaves, let them crackle for 10 seconds, then add the mustard seeds and let them do the same. Add the ground spices, toast in the hot oil for 30 seconds, then add the garlic and stir-fry for around 3 minutes, until sticky and golden.

Next add the can of tomatoes, breaking them up with the back of your spoon. Bring the sauce to a simmer, then add the lentils and 5½ cups of water, bring up to the boil, and reduce the heat to a gentle simmer. Cook for 30 minutes, stirring occasionally to make sure the lentils don't stick to the bottom of the pan. Once cooked, add 1¼ teaspoons of salt and the remaining 4 teaspoons of tamarind paste and simmer for a minute more. The texture of the rasam should be somewhere between a soup and a dal.

Cut each quarter of cabbage into 2 or 3 slices. Ladle the rasam into shallow bowls, place a couple of slices of cabbage on top, and serve alongside some steamed or boiled basmati rice if you like.

ROASTED SUNCHOKE AND CHICKPEA CHAAT

Chaat, for the uninitiated, means "to lick" but translates as that sort of lip-smacking street food for which you would travel across a city, climb a mosque, and crawl under an elephant. As every Indian knows, the best chaats are all about the chutneys.

note / You'll need to hop into an Indian supermarket to pick up the chaat masala and the sev (freeze any left over). You'll also need a blender. There's no need to peel the sunchokes if they're scrubbed well. Use a non-dairy yogurt if vegan.

Serves 4 /

2 lbs sunchokes, scrubbed and cut into 1-inch pieces

canola oil

salt

2½ cups mint leaves

¾ cup roughly chopped cilantro, plus handful of intact leaves

1½ green finger (or serrano) chiles, finely chopped

1 tbsp lemon juice

2 tbsp date syrup

2 tbsp tamarind paste

¼ tsp red chile powder, such as Kashmiri

½ cup plain yogurt, non-dairy if vegan

1 medium red onion, very finely chopped

1 x 14-oz can of chickpeas, drained

¾ inch ginger, peeled and very finely chopped

2–4 tsp chaat masala

a handful of sev (chickpea noodles) or Bombay mix, to serve

Preheat the oven to 475°F. Place the sunchokes on a baking sheet, then pour over 2½ tablespoons of oil and sprinkle over ¼ teaspoon of salt. Use your hands to coat them in the oil, then bake for 20 minutes, or until soft and a knife slips through them easily.

To make the mint and cilantro chutney, put the mint leaves and the chopped cilantro into a blender with ¼ cup of oil, 1 green chile, the lemon juice, and ¼ teaspoon of salt. Blend until smooth, then transfer to a small serving bowl. For the tamarind chutney, mix the date syrup, tamarind, and chile powder in another small bowl. Put the yogurt into a third small bowl with 2 pinches of salt and just enough water so that you are able to drizzle it.

Set aside 1 tablespoon of the onion to garnish. Place the sunchokes and chickpeas in a bowl and lightly mash using a fork, then add the remaining onion, the ginger, and half a green chile and mix well. Put 2 tablespoons of canola oil into a large non-stick frying pan over a medium heat and, when hot, add the sunchoke and chickpea mix. Cook for 10 minutes, stirring just once halfway through, to get some good char on the vegetables. Add 2 teaspoons of chaat masala, taste, and add up to 2 teaspoons more if you like, a little at a time. Mix well and tip onto a serving plate.

Drizzle over some of the mint and cilantro chutney, followed by the same amount of tamarind and yogurt. You won't need all of it—leave some so that people can customize their own bowls. Sprinkle a generous handful of sev over the top, followed by the remaining cilantro leaves and onion.

CHICKPEA FLOUR FRIES with chile sauce   V

The idea for these chickpea fries came to me when experimenting with the innovative Burmese chickpea tofu called "Shan tofu," which is made by cooking chickpea flour and water, then allowing it to set until hard enough to cut. The result can be sliced into strips and thrown into salads, or fried, a bit like normal tofu.

Serves 4 /

Scant 1 cup (7 oz) chickpea flour (gram flour)
½ tsp ground turmeric
1⅛ tsp salt
2 tbsp polenta
2 tbsp canola oil

For the chile sauce /
2 tbsp ketchup
2 tbsp sriracha

Line an 8-inch x 8-inch square baking pan with parchment paper.

In a large saucepan, whisk the flour, turmeric, salt, and ¾ cup of water until smooth. Leave to rest for 5 minutes, then whisk in a further 1¾ cup of water, and place the pan over a medium-high heat. Let it come to the boil, whisking continuously, as it is prone to sticking. When it boils, and the batter thickens, reduce the heat to low and simmer for 12 minutes—stirring all the while with a wooden spoon so the mixture doesn't stick and burn—until it's very thick and coming away from the bottom of the pan.

Pour the chickpea batter into the lined pan, lay a piece of parchment paper over the top, and smooth it down with your hands—do this fairly quickly as the batter will become hard to work with as it cools. Leave for 10 minutes to cool, then place in the fridge for at least an hour. While it sets, prepare the sauce by mixing the ketchup and sriracha together.

To cook the chickpea fries, lift the cooled, set batter out of the dish and place on a chopping board. Cut the batter in half, then cut each half into ½-inch-thick fries. Place the polenta on a plate and toss the fries in it until coated. Heat the oil in a large frying pan over a medium-high flame and add the fries in a single layer (you may need to fry them in batches, so as not to overcrowd the pan). Fry for 5 minutes, turning halfway through, until they are a lovely golden brown.

Serve the chickpea fries in a delicious pile next to a pool of the chile sauce.

AMRITSARI POMEGRANATE CHICKPEAS ⅴ

My trip to Amritsar will always be remembered for one thing: just how cold it was. My mistake wasn't wearing the wrong clothing, it was booking a hotel room with a three-inch gap under the door that let in the freezing temperatures. In lieu of central heating, the only way to stay warm was to visit the food-stall dhabas. We would stand by the tandoors, order bottomless chai, and fill our bellies with spicy chickpeas.

Two things distinguish this dish, known as "chole," from other Indian chickpea dishes. It is darker in color (which comes partly from the spices but mainly from the tea the chickpeas are boiled in), and it has a sour edge, from the pomegranate. Dried pomegranate seeds are used traditionally, but because they can be hard to come by, I use pomegranate molasses instead.

Serves 4 /

1 tsp cumin seeds

1 tsp fennel seeds

1 tsp coriander seeds

2 x 14-oz cans of chickpeas, drained

2 black teabags

3 tbsp canola oil

2 medium red onions, finely chopped

1¼ tsp salt

4 cloves of garlic, crushed

1 green finger (or serrano) chile, finely chopped

½ lb ripe tomatoes, chopped

1 tbsp pomegranate molasses

fresh cilantro leaves, to serve

Place a wide-bottomed frying pan over a medium heat. When hot, put the cumin, fennel, and coriander seeds into the pan and toast them for 4 minutes, or until almond-skin brown, stirring frequently. Bash using a pestle and mortar until fairly well ground, then leave to one side, keeping the pan for later.

Place the chickpeas in a medium-sized saucepan, add the teabags and a quart of water, and simmer for 20 minutes, until the chickpeas are soft and brown. Drain, remove and discard the teabags, and leave the chickpeas to one side.

Put the frying pan back on the heat, add the oil, and, when hot, put the chopped onions and salt into the pan. Cook for around 10 minutes, until soft and sweet, then add the garlic, chile, and ground spices and cook for 3 minutes. Add the chopped tomatoes and cook for a further 10 minutes, until you have a thick, dark paste, then add the pomegranate molasses, chickpeas, and 1¾ cups of hand-hot or freshly boiled water. Mash some of the chickpeas with a fork, to help the sauce thicken. Simmer for 10 minutes or so, until the sauce thickens a little more, then take off the heat. Transfer to a bowl and top with the fresh cilantro.

MAHAM'S DAL

V

One of the many things I love about the Pakistani ceramicist Maham Anjum is her hands. They move with incredible and well-practiced grace on her wheel, molding large, unfriendly-looking boulders of clay into elegant, perfectly formed bowls and biryani pots. I love her studio too, a rickety wooden shed in the midst of an overgrown garden full of foxgloves, butterflies, and a naughty little fox in the summer. I also loved this dal she served when I came to visit, which she introduced simply by saying: "I just put it all in a pot, Meera, and stir it."

note / This dal is made with the very quick-cooking "mung dal," which are the de-husked and split yellow insides of green mung beans. Bags of mung dal can be found in Indian stores.

Serves 4 /

For the dal /

1½ cups mung dal

½ lb ripe tomatoes, chopped

3 fat cloves of garlic, crushed

1 inch ginger, peeled and grated

½ tsp ground turmeric

1 tsp chile flakes

For the spiced oil /

3 tbsp canola oil

10 fresh curry leaves

1½ tsp salt

½ tsp black mustard seeds

1 tsp cumin seeds

1 green finger (or serrano) chile, very finely chopped

a handful of fresh cilantro, chopped

Put the mung dal, tomatoes, garlic, ginger, turmeric, and chile flakes into a large saucepan for which you have a lid, with 1 tablespoon of oil, 4 of the curry leaves, and 5¼ cups of water. Place on a medium heat, with the lid ajar, bring to the boil, then turn down to a simmer. Cook for 30 to 40 minutes, stirring every now and then, until it's soft and fairly thick, then stir in the salt.

To make the spiced oil, heat 2 tablespoons of oil in a small frying pan over a medium flame and, when smoking hot, add the mustard and cumin seeds, the chile, and the remaining 6 curry leaves. When the leaves crisp up and the seeds crackle, which should take about a minute, take the tarka off the heat and pour into the dal pan. Stir to mix, sprinkle over the cilantro, and serve with freshly steamed basmati rice.

sides

Growing up, there were no sides; there was no main thing at the center of the table, no hierarchy between dishes. Instead, there was simply a variety of delicious things to eat: usually a couple of vegetable curries and a dal, a pilau, yogurt, and a tray of pickles to jazz things up.

This simple arrangement belied a multitude of textures and temperatures: hot chiles against cold yogurt; sour pickles against soothing dal. Each dish had a role to play.

Sides were something that we ate in restaurants or at friends' houses, the side playing second fiddle to the prized meat at the center of the table. Today, the rules are changing, both in how restaurants choose to feed us and how we choose to feed ourselves.

The template of starters, mains, and sides is being ripped up, and we're freeing ourselves to eat in ways that feel right. Sides are being elevated and appreciated—sometimes even stealing the show. I love this change—and it's why I wanted to dedicate a chapter to these often neglected dishes.

Just treat these recipes as very useful tools in your culinary toolbox, and the world is your oyster (mushroom).

ROAST GREEN BEANS AND BROCCOLINI with sesame sauce

V

My husband and I disagree on how long to cook broccolini. I like it boiled to the point where it submits to the tooth (al dente), but he likes it quite crunchy. The only time we both agree is when it is roasted, as in this recipe. Roasting blackens and blisters the greens, while keeping the insides tender and bright. Although this recipe is a perfectly reasonable portion for 4 people, we can eat the whole thing between the two of us.

This dish is a loose spin on Japanese goma-ae, or greens served with a sesame sauce, where the seeds are ground and mixed with other ingredients, then tossed through the greens. I have cheated here a little by using tahini. This dish goes well with tofu and noodle dishes.

Serves 4 /

For the sauce /
¼ cup tahini
1 tbsp toasted sesame oil
1½ tbsp soy sauce
1 tbsp agave syrup
½ inch ginger, peeled and grated

For the greens /
2 tbsp canola oil
¼ tsp salt
⅔ lb broccolini
⅔ lb green beans, trimmed
1 tbsp black sesame seeds

Preheat the oven to 425°F.

Place all the ingredients for the sauce in a bowl and mix together, then add a little water to help loosen it up, so you can just about drizzle it.

For the greens, combine the oil and salt together in a tiny bowl, put the broccolini and green beans in a larger bowl, then pour over the oil and salt and mix it in well with your hands. You want to get the oil into the florets so that they don't burn too much.

Put the vegetables on a sheet pan and roast for 10 minutes, until charred. Remove to a big plate or platter, drizzle over the sauce, then sprinkle over the black sesame seeds.

SICHUAN EGGPLANT

V

There are six territories within China, each with different culinary traditions, but my love for Sichuanese food burns the brightest. This is partly because of how unsubtle, unrestrained, and garlicky it is, but also because I love the names of the dishes, which sound as if they're out of a Grimm's fairy tale. These eggplants are usually called "fish fragrant"—not because they contain any fish, but because they are cooked with the same ingredients used to cook seafood: fermented chile bean sauce, garlic, and ginger, creating layers of wonderful flavors. This dish works well with other Sichuan-style dishes like the mushroom mapo tofu on page 171 and kung pao cauliflower on page 235.

Serves 4 /

3 small eggplants (2 lbs)

2 tbsp canola oil

¾ inch ginger, peeled and grated

3 cloves of garlic, grated

2 tsp sugar

1 tbsp Chinkiang black vinegar

2 tbsp chile bean sauce (see page 287)

1 tsp cornstarch

1 cup vegan vegetable stock

salt, to taste

4 green onions, sliced into long, thin strips

Trim the eggplants, then quarter them lengthways and cut each piece in half widthways to give roughly 1½-inch-long pieces. Place these in a bowl, add the oil, and mix well to ensure that each piece is well coated.

Put a large non-stick frying pan over a medium-high heat and, when hot, place the eggplant in the pan flesh side down. Don't overcrowd the pan: do this in batches to ensure the eggplant cooks in a single layer. Cook each batch for around 6 to 8 minutes, turning them over every 2 minutes, until golden tender and cooked through, then remove to a plate.

In a small bowl, mix together the ginger, garlic, sugar, vinegar, chile bean sauce, and cornstarch, then add a few tablespoons of the stock to loosen.

Set the same pan over a medium heat and add the sauce and the remaining stock. Bring to the boil, then turn the heat down to a gentle simmer and cook for around 3 minutes, just long enough for the sauce to thicken and coat the back of a spoon. Return the eggplant to the pan and mix well with the sauce: you want each piece of eggplant to be wearing a silky jacket of the ruby-red sauce. Simmer for another minute, then remove from the heat. Taste and add salt if need be, then transfer to a serving dish and scatter over the green onions.

KUNG PAO CAULIFLOWER

V

Sticky, sweet, hot, and packed with crunchy peanuts, kung pao is a Western remix of a Sichuanese dish called gong bao. This dish goes well with Sichuan eggplant (see page 232) and steamed jasmine rice.

Serves 4 as part of a larger meal /

2 lbs (1 large) cauliflower

1 tsp Sichuan peppercorns

canola oil

2 tsp cornstarch

2½ tbsp soy sauce

1½ tbsp white wine vinegar

2 tbsp hoisin sauce

⅓ tsp salt

4 green onions, very finely chopped, whites and greens separated

4 cloves of garlic, sliced paper thin

4 bird's-eye chiles, slit lengthways

¾ inch ginger, peeled and sliced into thin batons

⅓ cup unsalted peanuts

Preheat the oven to 425°F.

Trim the cauliflower and break down into bite-size florets, around 1½ inches at the widest part, then place on your largest baking sheet in a single layer. The pieces should not overlap (or they'll steam), so use two pans if you need to.

Smash the Sichuan peppercorns with a pestle and mortar until well ground, then add 2 tablespoons of oil to the mortar, mix well, and pour over the cauliflower, rubbing the oil and pepper into the florets thoroughly until coated. Place in the oven and roast for 20 minutes or until tender and beginning to char, turning the florets over halfway through.

In the meantime, make the sauce. Put the cornstarch into a bowl and slowly mix in the soy sauce, ensuring there are no lumps, followed by the vinegar, hoisin sauce, and salt. Make sure you have all the other ingredients prepared and within arm's reach, for the next step.

Put 2 tablespoons of oil into a large non-stick frying pan on a high heat. When smoking hot, add the roasted cauliflower and toss for a minute, then add the green onion whites, the garlic, chiles, and ginger. Cook for 3 to 4 minutes, stirring only every minute or so to help char the mixture. Then add the sauce and cook for 3 to 4 minutes, stirring occasionally, until dark, sticky, and glossy. Toss through the peanuts, then tip onto a serving plate, sprinkle over the rest of the green onion, and serve.

NEW POTATO SERUNDENG   V

I'm excited to introduce you to serundeng, an Indonesian condiment and a gift to every home cook who is looking to liven up a dish. Affectionately known as "crispy bits" in the Sodha household, these bits are made by frying coconut, shallots, garlic, and tamarind until they give up their very best flavors and become crunchy enough to top salads, rice, or, in this case, new potatoes. Although it might look like a lot of salt to boil the potatoes in, they absorb only a little—just enough to be perfectly seasoned.

As this is quite a dry side dish, it's best paired with a dish with sauce, for example the tempeh with bok choy and tomato sambal on page 168, or the nutmeg, lime, and coconut green beans on page 245.

Serves 4 /

1¾ lbs new potatoes, scrubbed
  if necessary

salt

canola oil

2 large shallots, very finely chopped

3 cloves of garlic, crushed

½ tsp ground cumin

1 tsp ground coriander

2 tsp tamarind paste

⅓ cup dried shredded coconut

½ cup unsalted peanuts

Put the potatoes, 1 tablespoon of salt, and 6½ cups of water into a medium-sized saucepan. Set over a high heat, bring to the boil, and cook for 15 to 25 minutes (depending on the size of your potatoes), until a knife slides in with no resistance. Drain well, tip back into the pan, and put on the lowest heat possible for a couple of minutes, to allow them to dry out a little.

While the potatoes are cooking, make the serundeng. Heat 1½ table-spoons of oil over a high heat in a frying pan, then add the shallots and garlic and cook for 5 minutes, stirring frequently, until the shallots are starting to color at the edges. Add the cumin, coriander, ½ teaspoon of salt, and the tamarind and cook for 2 minutes, then add the coconut and peanuts. Mix well, turn the heat down, and cook for another 5 minutes, stirring frequently, until the mixture is brown and crispy.

When the potatoes are cooked, drain and tip them onto a serving platter, drizzle with oil, top with the serundeng, and serve.

ROASTED CARROTS AND CABBAGE
with gochujang

V

Take your carrots and cabbage to Seoul and back. It's worth the trip.

Serves 4 /

1⅔ lbs carrots, peeled and quartered

1⅔ lbs green cabbage, cut into
 ¾-inch wedges

1½ tbsp gochujang paste

1 tsp ground cumin

1¼ tsp salt

4 cloves of garlic, crushed

1 inch ginger, peeled and grated

canola oil

1 tbsp white wine vinegar

Preheat the oven to 425°F and line two large sheet pans with foil.

Place the carrots in one pan and the cabbage in another. In a small bowl, mix the gochujang, cumin, salt, garlic, ginger, and 3 tablespoons of oil. Pour half across each pan of vegetables, and mix with your hands so that the marinade gets everywhere. Make sure the carrots and cabbage are in a single layer, then place the pans in the oven for 35 to 40 minutes, until the vegetables are tender and blackened at the edges.

Meanwhile, put 2 tablespoons of oil and the white wine vinegar into a large bowl. When the carrots and cabbage are roasted, transfer them to the bowl while still hot and toss them in the oil and vinegar. Pile the vegetables onto a large plate and serve.

ROASTED CARROTS AND CABBAGE

TANDOORI BROCCOLI

The tandoor has been around for over 5,000 years, but you will struggle to find one in an Indian home as this ancient clay oven remains the reserve of restaurants, cafes, and makeshift street-food stalls. In most of the Western world, things are different. Ovens are commonplace and, with the press of a few buttons, we can bring their heat to anything and everything. In this recipe I've given broccoli the classic tandoori marinade makeover and it suits it. The key to this dish is to work the marinade into the florets but not to overdo it. Charring the broccoli will bring out a fantastic contrasting bitter edge to the creamy marinade.

Serves 6 /

canola oil

2 broccoli heads (1 lb)

1 cup full-fat cream cheese

1 tbsp lemon juice

3 cloves of garlic, crushed

1 inch ginger, peeled and grated

1¼ tsp red chile powder, such as Kashmiri

1¼ tsp salt

1 tsp garam masala

Preheat the oven to 425°F, line two baking sheets with foil, and brush a little oil over the foil.

Turn the broccoli heads upside down and carefully quarter them lengthways. Mix all the other ingredients together in a bowl and push the mixture into the nooks and crannies of the broccoli florets with your hands, leaving the stems bare.

Put a little oil into the same bowl and, using a pastry brush, brush the stems with the oil. Spread the quarters out across the pans and bake for 20 minutes, or until the stalks are tender and the florets are a burnished red. Transfer to a dish, and serve.

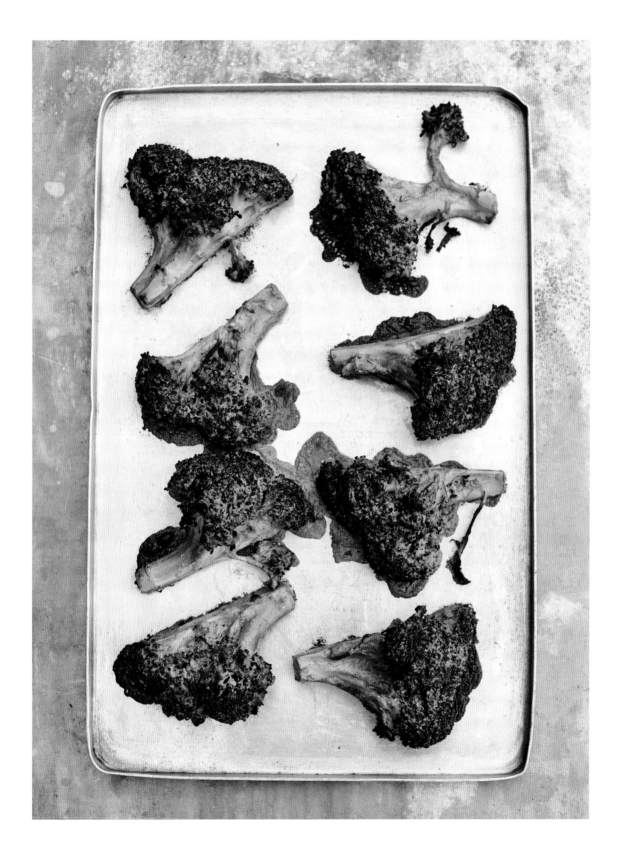

TAMARIND SHALLOTS

There's much more than meets the eye with the shallot. Roast those pretty petals and you'll find some of the richest, sweetest flavors you'll taste in the natural world. In this recipe, the shallots are roasted with sweet tomatoes and then mixed with tamarind. They're a wonderful side to have with a gentle dish, in particular the new potato and green bean istoo on page 112 (see also the photo there).

Serves 4 /

1¾ lbs shallots

¾ lb ripe tomatoes

1 tsp cumin seeds

½ tsp black mustard seeds

5 tbsp canola oil

¾ tsp salt

2 tsp tamarind paste

8 fresh curry leaves

1 green finger (or serrano) chile, halved

Preheat the oven to 400°F and line two large baking sheets with foil.

Trim the tops and bottoms of the shallots and separate the cloves, if there are any. Peel and halve lengthwise. Place the shallots on one of the pans, unfurling some of the petals as you go (only enough to fill the baking pan in one layer; you don't want the shallots to sit on top of one another). Halve the tomatoes and place on the other pan.

Using a pestle and mortar, grind together the cumin and mustard seeds until you have a coarse powder. Add the oil and salt, stir, then pour over the shallots and tomatoes and mix with your hands, making sure the vegetables are well coated with the spices and oil.

Bake for 25 minutes, turning the pans around halfway through. Remove from the oven, tip the tomatoes into the shallot pan, and add the tamarind, curry leaves, and chile. Carefully mix using a wooden spoon, then bake for another 5 to 8 minutes, until they're starting to blacken and char in places. Transfer to a bowl to serve.

NUTMEG, LIME, AND COCONUT GREEN BEANS

V

This side dish goes well with just about anything, but is particularly good with the new potato serundeng on page 237.

Serves 4 /

2 tbsp canola oil

1 medium red onion, very finely chopped

3 cloves of garlic, crushed

½ inch ginger, peeled and finely grated

1 bird's-eye chile, finely chopped

½ tsp salt

1 tsp sugar

1 lb green beans, trimmed

1 cup coconut cream

1 whole nutmeg (or ¼ tsp ground nutmeg)

1 lime, quartered

Put the oil into a large frying pan for which you have a lid, and place over a medium heat. When hot, add the onion and cook for 6 minutes, stirring frequently, until starting to brown, then add the garlic, ginger, and chile. Cook for 4 minutes, then add the salt and sugar, stir, and add the beans. Pour over the coconut cream and stir again.

Turn the heat down to low and cook for 8 to 10 minutes, or until the coconut cream is driven off (it will turn from milky to clear), leaving a transparent, silky mess of green beans. Take them off the heat, grate over roughly a third of the whole nutmeg (or add the ground nutmeg), then squeeze over a lime quarter, mix, and taste—you may like to add a little more lime.

Transfer to a serving platter, slice the remaining lime quarters in two, and place alongside for people to each help themselves if they wish.

BLACKENED CORN with miso butter

I believe miso butter came from the wonderful mind of Momofuku's David Chang. But I can't hold him responsible for this recipe, in which I've used gochujang (see page 288) to bring a little sweet heat to the game and lime to cut everything down to size. You can make the corn as you like: boil it or BBQ it. My personal preference is to cook it over a gas burner on the lowest flame, controlling how it blackens using a pair of tongs.

You can serve this dish as an appetizer, or alongside other BBQ dishes—or slice off the kernels, mix into the miso butter, and serve alongside a rice dish, like the Brussels sprout nasi goreng on page 132.

Serves 4 as an appetizer or side /

4 corn cobs, dehusked
1 lime, cut into wedges

For the miso butter /
2 tbsp unsalted butter
¼ cup white miso
½ tsp red chile powder, such as Kashmiri
2 tsp gochujang paste
1 green onion, very finely sliced
salt, to taste

Take the corn out of the fridge 15 minutes before cooking so that it comes up to room temperature.

Strip the corn of any silky strands and turn a burner on a gas stove to the smallest flame. Keep a plate to one side and, using a pair of heatproof tongs, hold the corn over the heat. Cook each cob for 5 to 8 minutes, turning every 30 seconds, until the kernels are a deep yellow or charred black. Place the cooked cobs on the plate and leave until cool enough to handle.

Meanwhile, make the miso butter. Put the butter and miso into a small saucepan with the chile powder, gochujang, and green onion, and cook over a low heat until the butter has melted. Stir to mix, and taste for salt—mine needed a pinch; yours might too.

You can slice the kernels off the corn cobs if you prefer, or put the whole cobs on a serving plate. Pour over the hot miso butter, and serve immediately with the lime wedges to squeeze over.

WHOLE ROAST SQUASH

WHOLE ROAST SQUASH
with black bean and chile oil

V

There have been times when, despite the size of my knife, I haven't been able to saw my way into a thick-skinned squash or pumpkin. But my lack of success led me to another idea: roast it whole. I've since done so many times—creating an impossibly creamy, sweet mash, without having to do any mashing.

You may need to go to an Asian supermarket or look online to find the salted fermented black beans. They are the Asian equivalent of an anchovy or olive, and really worth knowing about. Their natural flavor is incomparable with the sickly-sweet black bean sauces that come in jars and, as an added bonus, a bag of these beans will live almost indefinitely in your cupboard.

Serves 6 /

1 x 3½ lbs squash, such as kabocha, pricked with a fork

2 tbsp canola oil

¼ tsp salt

For the black bean and chile oil /

2 tbsp canola oil

3 cloves of garlic, finely sliced

1 tbsp salted fermented black beans, rinsed

2 tsp chile flakes

1 tbsp soy sauce

1 tsp sugar

Preheat the oven to 400°F.

Place the squash in a roasting pan and cook in the oven for 1 to 1½ hours, until very soft and just starting to collapse a little at the belly.

While the squash cooks, make your black bean and chile oil. In a small saucepan, heat 2 tablespoons of canola oil over a low flame for 1 minute. Add the garlic to the oil and fry gently for 1 to 2 minutes, until golden brown and sticky. Remove the pan from the heat to let the oil cool a little and carefully add the black beans. Return to the heat and add the chile flakes, soy sauce, 2 tablespoons of water, and the sugar. Cook for a further 30 seconds, stirring constantly, then remove from the heat and allow to cool.

When cool enough to touch, slice the squash in half. Using your hand like a bear's paw, claw out the seeds from the middle of the squash (or scoop out using a spoon) and discard. Scoop out the flesh and place in a bowl with the remaining 2 tablespoons of canola oil and the salt. Beat with a fork until the squash is very smooth, then spread onto a plate. Make a shallow well in the center, pour in the black bean and chile oil, and serve.

condiments

Most people hang a meal around a main course, but I could start with condiments first. This is where my dopamine hits lie, in the hot, sweet fire of a jar of chile oil or the salty, pungent cream of kimchi mayonnaise. For me, everything else fades away on the plate when a pickle appears.

There are many recipes for sauces and chutneys woven through this book, all of which can be repurposed and used as you wish (see a reminder of these below). However, in this chapter you'll find some very exciting but easy essentials to perk up any meal.

A reminder of other sauces, chutneys, and pickles in the book:

Kimchi mayo (page 22) / Walnut miso (page 25) / Wasabi mayo (page 202) / Miso butter (page 246) / Ponzu sauce (page 49) / Gochujang sauce (page 148) / Okonomiyaki sauce (page 201) / Chile sauce (page 225) / Sesame sauce (page 230) / Black bean and chile oil (page 251) / Pea and coconut chutney (page 32) / Cabbage pickle (page 81) / Pickled radishes (page 105) / Pickled cucumber (page 135) / Lemon pickle (page 186)

KECAP MANIS

HOT CASHEW SAUCE

SICHUAN CHILE OIL

VEGAN MAYONNAISE

CARROT ACHAR

PICKLED GINGER

VEGAN MAYONNAISE   V

If you've ever handled silken tofu and put a gently wobbling square of it in your mouth to see how it melts when probed with the tongue, you could see how it could easily be transformed into a lovely silky mayonnaise. As tofus vary a little in taste, I think a vegan "mayonnaise" should always have a little extra help, in the form of Dijon mustard, garlic, and lemon juice, to get things moving.

note / You'll need a blender for this recipe.

Makes 8 oz /

8 oz silken tofu, well drained / 1½ tsp lemon juice / 1½ tsp white wine vinegar / ½ tsp salt / ½ tsp Dijon mustard / ½ tsp sugar / ½ a clove of garlic, finely chopped / ¼ cup canola oil

This couldn't be simpler. Combine all the ingredients in a blender and blitz for a full minute until you have a smooth, thick, and glossy mayonnaise. Check the mayonnaise for seasoning, adjusting the salt and lemon juice as you see fit, and store in the fridge for up to a week.

PICKLED GINGER   V

There is a whole universe of Japanese vegetable pickles known as tsukemono, but one of my favorites is beni shoga: thin strips of ginger traditionally pickled in the pickling liquid for Japanese plums, making it bright pink. It's often found dancing on yaki udon (see my udon noodles with red cabbage and cauliflower, page 88) or okonomiyaki. Sadly this one is not bright pink as I didn't want to complicate the recipe—but you could add a little beet powder if that's your thing.

Makes 2½ tbsp /

2 inches ginger, peeled and cut into tiny batons / ¼ tsp salt / 4½ tsp white wine vinegar / 4 tsp sugar

Mix the batons of ginger with the salt in a small bowl and leave to rest for 30 minutes, then squeeze well to remove as much water as possible.

Combine the vinegar, sugar, and 1 tablespoon of water in a small pan. Heat over a low flame until the sugar is dissolved, add the squeezed ginger, and leave to cool. Transfer to a sterilized container and put it in the fridge, where it will keep for up to a month.

HOT CASHEW SAUCE

V

Forgive me, for I have repurposed a recipe. I originally created this for a Mexican chipotle sauce in the *Guardian*, but I enjoyed it so much that I thought it would be useful to include a variation of it in this book. I've used red chile powder here to create a gently hot sauce which is perfect for sandwiches, salad dressings, and most things you could imagine putting a creamy hot sauce over.

Makes ¾ cup /

¾ cup unsalted cashews / 1 clove of garlic / 2 tbsp canola oil / ½ tsp salt / 1 tsp red chile powder, such as Kashmiri

Place the cashews in a saucepan and cover with 1¼ cups of water. Bring to the boil, then turn the heat to low and simmer for 10 minutes. Peel the garlic clove, throw it into the pan, turn off the heat, and leave to cool.

When cool, put the contents of the pan into a blender with the oil, salt, and chile powder, and blitz to a smooth sauce. Scrape into a bottle, cup, or bowl, and store in the fridge for up to a week.

KECAP MANIS

V

Most recipes suggest making a simple syrup out of soy and sugar, but I found that by the time I had boiled it down it was unbearably salty. My recipe requires just mixing agave syrup with soy. I've used dark soy because it has a much deeper molasses flavor, which normal soy does not have. Scale up as you need.

Makes just over 1 tbsp /

1 tbsp agave syrup /
1 tsp dark soy sauce

Place the two sauces into a small bowl and mix.

SICHUAN CHILE OIL

Sichuan chile oil is a beautiful chorus of garlic, chile, spices, and sesame. These few ingredients, gently infused in oil in a matter of minutes, provide a jar of gentle fire ready to throw into dishes from congee to ramen, noodles to plain rice.

You can buy chile oils from large supermarkets and Asian markets that are really delicious, but this homemade version easily measures up to them. It's quick, uses predominantly pantry ingredients, and will make you feel wonderfully accomplished.

note / You'll need a blender for this recipe.

Makes 1 cup /

1 tbsp Sichuan peppercorns /
1 cup canola oil / 1 tsp ground
cumin / 1 bird's-eye chile, finely
chopped / 2 cloves of garlic, crushed
or grated / 2 tbsp chile flakes /
¼ tsp salt / ¾ tsp sugar / 1 tbsp
toasted sesame oil / 1½ tsp soy
sauce

Grind the Sichuan peppercorns using a pestle and mortar, until you have a rough powder. Put the ground Sichuan peppercorns into a small saucepan and add all the other ingredients except the sesame oil and the soy sauce. Place over a very low heat and leave the ingredients to get to know one another for 5 minutes. Toward the end of the time it should be gently sizzling.

Remove the pan from the heat and allow to cool for 5 minutes. Add the sesame oil and soy sauce and stir well to combine, then allow to cool fully. The oil will keep in an airtight jar in the fridge for around a month.

CARROT ACHAR

V

A great little pickle is worthy of a spot in your fridge. It will perk up curries, dals, rice, and sandwiches. An all-carrot version of this is good for some color-blocking on the table, but it also works with green beans, turnip, kohlrabi—and, I daresay, other vegetables too.

Makes a large jar (around 16 oz) /

1 tsp coriander seeds

1 tsp cumin seeds

1 tsp black mustard seeds

1 inch ginger, peeled and roughly chopped

4 cloves of garlic, roughly chopped

2 green finger (or serrano) chiles, roughly chopped

⅓ cup canola oil

10 fresh curry leaves

a pinch of fenugreek seeds

1 lb carrots, peeled and cut into slim 1½-inch batons

1 tsp ground turmeric

1½ tsp salt

½ tsp sugar

¼ cup white wine vinegar

Grind the coriander, cumin, and mustard seeds using a pestle and mortar until you have a coarse powder. Scoop out of the mortar and set aside. Use the pestle and mortar to bash the ginger, garlic, chiles, and 2 tablespoons of water until you have a rough paste.

Heat the oil in a large frying pan for which you have a lid, and add the curry leaves. When they crackle and turn emerald green, add the crushed seeds and the fenugreek seeds. Stir for 2 minutes, then add the garlic, ginger, and chile paste. Cook for 5 minutes until the oil starts to separate from the paste, stirring regularly so that it doesn't catch, then add the carrots, turmeric, salt, sugar, and vinegar. Put the lid on and cook for 10 minutes, or until the carrots are tender. Remove the lid and cook for another 5 minutes, being careful that the spices don't burn.

Taste and adjust the seasoning as you see fit—you may like to add a little more salt, sugar, or vinegar—then take off the heat. When cooled, transfer to a clean jar and pop into the fridge. Eat within a couple of weeks.

sweet

So much of our culinary pleasure comes from having food just the way we like it.

For years, I didn't like Indian sweets. I learned to duck and swerve Indian aunties at every festival, wedding, and birthday, their hands poised at mouth level ready to launch a small barfi, cham cham, or piece of sandesh into my mouth. For my hybrid palate, with half my taste buds in England and the other in India, the sugar felt brash, the flavors heavy-handed, and the textures too dense.

This hasn't resulted in a blanket ban, and there are a couple of traditional Indian desserts in this chapter: a heavenly stove-top rice pudding made with basmati rice; and a sweet strained yogurt called "shrikhand" that's so creamy and thick you could stand a spoon up in it.

What I really love, however—much like the Victorians did—is the liberal use of spice in desserts. Just as sugar and spice can transform tea into a steamy magical chai, spices can really make a dessert jump from the "quite nice" category into something to desire with an unholy passion.

Also, as you will see in this chapter, there is quite a bit of fruit and a little chocolate. This is because, no matter which world cuisine you happen to be eating, fruit and chocolate are a universally excellent way to finish a meal. So here are a few favorites—from all over.

SUNKEN GINGER PLUM AND SPELT CAKE

Ginger and plum are a fine pair of ingredients, often found lounging around together in a Chinese sauce. Although they are both able to carry a cake by themselves, when combined they make for a boldly flavored, jammy, pudding-like cake. I've used spelt instead of all-purpose flour, because it boasts a nutty flavor and better credentials in the nutrient department, but you could use all-purpose if you can't find spelt.

note / The applesauce adds moisture to compensate for the lack of eggs, but for a non-vegan version use 2 large eggs in place of the ground flaxseeds and almond milk, and soft unsalted butter instead of the non-dairy spread. This can be eaten hot or cold, though it's best warm, with a little yogurt, ice cream, or cream (dairy-free, if you are vegan).

Serves 8 /

2 tbsp ground flaxseeds

⅓ cup unsweetened almond milk

8 tbsp (½ cup) non-dairy spread

⅓ cup dark brown sugar, plus extra for sprinkling

⅓ cup unsweetened applesauce

½ tsp vanilla extract

¾ cup + 1 tbsp white spelt flour

½ cup almond flour

1 tsp baking powder

½ tsp baking soda

1 tbsp + 1 tsp ground ginger

a pinch of salt

7 small firm plums (about ¾ lb), halved and pitted

Preheat the oven to 400°F and line an 8-inch cake pan with parchment paper. Mix the flaxseeds and almond milk in a small bowl.

Put the non-dairy spread, sugar, applesauce, and vanilla in a large bowl and vigorously mix with a hand whisk—it will look a little split, but that's OK. With a wooden spoon, fold in the spelt flour, almond flour, baking powder, baking soda, ginger, and salt, until just combined. Now add the flaxseed mixture, fold once more to combine, then pour into the prepared pan.

Top the batter with the plum halves, cut side up, overlapping them slightly as you go, then sprinkle over about a tablespoon of brown sugar. Bake for 40 minutes, turning the pan halfway through, until the top of the cake is firm to the touch, golden brown, and a skewer inserted into the center comes out clean. Leave to cool in the pan for a few minutes, then remove from the pan and serve warm.

PINEAPPLE LOVE CAKE

When I was growing up, our oven was used to store exiled chopping boards and frying pans. As a result, any cake that merited the annual clearing of the Sodha oven had to be incredibly special. One day, I found it: the mighty Sri Lankan love cake, whose origin dates back to the fifteenth century, when the Portuguese ruled parts of Ceylon. It's everything I love: dense, floral, and full of nuts and spices. This particular pineapple variation evolved when I cooked with Richard Blackwell, then head chef at the Dock Kitchen. It's a cake worth clearing out the oven for.

note / This is a vegan cake, but for a non-vegan version use 4 large eggs in place of the flaxseeds and almond milk, and soft unsalted butter instead of the non-dairy spread.

Serves 8 /

8 tbsp (½ cup) non-dairy spread, plus extra for greasing

¼ cup ground flaxseeds

¾ cup unsweetened almond milk

1 small pineapple, peeled

zest and juice of 1 orange (you should get ¼ cup of juice)

1¼ cups light brown sugar

1 tsp rose water extract or 2 tbsp rose water

1 tsp vanilla extract

zest of 1 lemon

Scant 1 cup almond flour

1¼ cup semolina flour

1½ tsp ground cinnamon

¼ tsp ground nutmeg

1 tsp ground cardamom

1 tsp baking powder

Preheat the oven to 400°F. Grease the base and sides of a 9-inch cake pan with non-dairy spread and line the base with parchment paper, making sure it comes at least 1 inch up the sides of the pan (so the juices don't leak). Mix the flaxseeds and almond milk in a small bowl.

Lie the pineapple on its side, cut 8 round ¼-inch-thick slices off the bottom and put into a saucepan. Add the orange juice and ¼ cup of the sugar, bring the mixture up to the boil, then turn off the heat and set aside.

In a bowl, use a spatula to cream the non-dairy spread and the remaining sugar in a large bowl, then mix in the rose water, vanilla extract, lemon zest, and orange zest. In a second bowl, whisk together the dry ingredients—the almond flour, semolina, cinnamon, nutmeg, cardamom, and baking powder. Add the flaxseed mixture to the creamed spread and sugar, then fold in the dry ingredients until just combined.

Layer the pineapple slices, one over another, in the base of the pan to form an interlocking circle with no hole in the middle, then pour the pan juices over the top. Spoon the cake batter into the pan over the pineapple, and use the back of a spoon to level it out. Bake for 45 minutes, or until a skewer comes out clean, then remove from the oven and leave to cool in the pan for 20 minutes. To turn out the cake, run a knife around the sides, put a plate on top of the pan, and turn over. Voila! Serve with non-dairy yogurt.

SAFFRON, ALMOND, AND LEMON CAKES

Some recipes are born out of a creative vision I have in the middle of the night, but these cakes came about because I had some egg whites to use up. I added some of my favorite sweet ingredients—saffron, almonds, and lemon—and out of the ashes the phoenix rose.

Makes 8 mini cakes /

For the cakes /

1¼ sticks (10 tbsp) unsalted butter

20 strands of saffron, plus a few more to decorate

1 cup almond flour

⅔ cup all-purpose flour

⅔ cup superfine sugar

a pinch of salt

4 egg whites

zest and juice of 1 lemon

For the frosting /

½ cup powdered sugar

½ stick (4 tbsp) unsalted butter, softened

½ cup + 1 tbsp (9 tbsp) full-fat cream cheese

Preheat the oven to 400°F and line a 12-hole muffin pan with eight paper cases.

Melt the butter in a small saucepan, then crumble the saffron between your fingers and add it to the butter to infuse. Put the flours, sugar, and salt into a mixing bowl and whisk together. Add the egg whites and beat well, then add the butter and saffron mixture, half the lemon zest, and half the lemon juice, mixing as you go. Spoon the batter into the cases, and bake for 15 minutes or until the cakes are golden and a skewer comes out clean. Remove from the oven and leave to cool completely.

To make the cream cheese frosting, beat the sugar with the butter until smooth, then fold in the cream cheese and the rest of the lemon zest and juice until just mixed. When the cakes are cool, spoon over the frosting. Use an offset spatula to smooth it around the top of each cake into a gentle cone, then, for a touch of glamour, place a single strand of saffron on top of each one.

VIETNAMESE COFFEE ICE CREAM

Vietnamese coffee is strong, sweet, and made with condensed milk, which gives it a rich, velvety smoothness. It made complete sense to transform it into a delicious post-dinner ice cream. As Mum makes her coffee ice cream using condensed milk and freezes it without churning (Indian women have always been so artful with cans of evaporated and condensed milk), I asked her for some advice. She said, "I got the recipe from Aunty Savi, beda [darling]. She got it from a friend of hers, who said she saw Nigella make it on the television." So with thanks (and apologies) to Nigella Lawson, here is my recipe for Vietnamese coffee ice cream, adapted from Mum's recipe, which is adapted from Aunty Savi, who got it from her friend, who originally got it from Nigella Lawson.

note / You'll need a deep, airtight 1-quart container for the ice cream.

Makes 1 quart /

¼ cup instant espresso coffee granules, plus ½ tsp to decorate

2½ cups heavy cream, divided

1 x 14-oz can of condensed milk

First make up the coffee. Place the coffee granules in a large heatproof bowl and pour over ¼ cup of boiled water. Stir to dissolve the granules, then pour in 1¼ cups heavy cream and the condensed milk and mix well.

In another large bowl, whip 1¼ cups heavy cream into soft peaks, so that when you lift the whisk, the cream does not fall back into the bowl. Slowly pour the coffee mixture into the whipped cream, stirring as you go, until completely combined.

Pour into your quart container, sprinkle with a few coffee granules, and pop into the freezer for at least 4 hours, until hard. Take the ice cream out of the freezer 5 minutes before you want to eat it. It scoops beautifully but melts very quickly, so pop the tub back into the freezer as soon as you've finished serving.

CARDAMOM KHEER

I take a bite of this sweet rice pudding and I am back at my parents' house at Diwali. They've just been dancing. Arya is eighteen months old, playing with the dancing stick and shrieking with laughter. One more spoonful, and she's six months old and just learning to eat; she doesn't wrinkle her nose at a simple kheer made with apples. A couple more spoonfuls and it's 2015, I'm in Bademiya in Mumbai, it's 2 a.m. and Hugh's just arrived. I've been away from him for weeks again, traveling to research recipes for *Fresh India*. I missed him so much I could barely eat, but now he's here and the kheer tastes like sweet celebration. Another spoonful and I'm six again, struggling to fit in at a new school. I don't tell Mum, but perhaps she knows because there's kheer for pudding and it tastes like home.

Serves 4 /

½ cup + 1 tbsp basmati rice

1 tsp ground cardamom

½ tsp ground cinnamon

scant ½ cup superfine sugar, plus 1 tbsp to decorate

3 cups whole milk, plus extra if needed

⅔ cup heavy cream

3 tbsp unsalted pistachios

1½ tbsp dried edible flowers (such as marigolds, roses, lavender)

Place the rice, spices, sugar, milk, and cream in a large saucepan and set over a medium-low heat. Bring to the boil—but watch it doesn't boil over—then turn the heat down to a whisper and cook for about 30 minutes, stirring fairly frequently to make sure the rice doesn't stick and burn. If the mixture is getting too dry, add more milk, a little at a time. When the rice is nearly done, it will start to bubble and burp more furiously and will need more attention from you. When the rice is tender (i.e. there's no chalkiness in the center), take it off the heat and spoon into a serving bowl. Allow to cool, then cover and chill in the fridge until cold.

Just before serving, grind the remaining tablespoon of sugar, the pistachios, and edible flowers as finely as you can, using a mortar and pestle or electric spice grinder. Sprinkle over the top, and serve.

STEM GINGER CHOCOLATE TRUFFLES   V

Every person knows their particular weakness. It could be a new pair of sneakers for some, a pint of Guinness for others, or the twopenny slot machines and a bag of doughnuts at the beach for my grandma. But for me, stem ginger enrobed in dark chocolate is an offer I cannot refuse.

Given my disposition, these are frustratingly simple to make. There is no need to set up a double boiler to melt the chocolate: simply chop it up and pour the other ingredients over it. Just remember to take it out of the fridge at least 10 minutes before serving to soften up a little.

note / You can buy stem ginger from the UK online.

Makes 25 /

11 oz vegan dark chocolate (70%)
¼ cup refined coconut oil
¼ cup + 1 tbsp almond butter
¼ cup stem ginger syrup
¼ cup chopped stem ginger
¼ cup candied ginger, roughly chopped

Line an 8-inch x 8-inch square pan with parchment paper. Roughly chop the chocolate into bite-size pieces and put it into a large heatproof bowl.

Place the coconut oil, almond butter, stem ginger syrup, and chopped stem ginger in a small pan over a low heat. When everything has melted (the almond butter may stay clumped up, but don't worry about this), pour it over the chocolate and stir with a fork to mix, breaking up any lumps of butter.

Pour the chocolate mixture into the prepared pan, gently shake to distribute evenly, and sprinkle over the candied ginger. Leave somewhere cool to set—or pop into the fridge, but take out 10 minutes before serving so it softens slightly. Cut into 25 squares when set.

BANANA BREAD with toasted coconut   V

While other treats come and go with seasons and flights of fancy, banana bread is steady—it's the safe bet and the crowd-pleaser, and also my secret favorite. Not all banana breads are created equal, however. This one is so dense, you could bite into a slice with your lips and it would remember them like memory foam. It's sweet, but not so sweet that it can't be eaten for breakfast with a choice spread (peanut butter) and jam. But it's still sweet enough to be eaten on its own, all year round and forever.

note / You'll need a 1-lb loaf pan and a food processor to make this. It needs to be left to rest in the pan until cool before slicing.

Serves 8 /

⅓ cup + 1 tbsp (7 tbsp) coconut oil, plus extra for greasing

scant ½ cup maple syrup

1 tsp vanilla extract

1¼ cups all-purpose flour

scant 1 cup ground almonds

1 cup dried shredded coconut

2 tsp baking powder

1½ tsp ground cinnamon

1 tsp ground nutmeg

1 lb ripe banana flesh (approx 2¼ cups of 1-inch chunks)

⅓ cup raw (untoasted) coconut chips

Preheat the oven to 400°F. Grease your loaf pan with coconut oil, then line the base with a long strip of parchment paper (this will make it easier to lift out the bread later).

In a small pan, heat the coconut oil until just melted, then take it off the heat, stir in the maple syrup and vanilla, and set aside. In a bowl, whisk together the flour, almonds, shredded coconut, baking powder, cinnamon, and nutmeg.

Put the banana into a food processor and blitz to a smooth puree. Add the flour mixture and oil to the banana, and process again until just combined. Scrape down the sides of the processor and pulse once more. Scrape the mixture into the pan and spread it out evenly. Sprinkle with enough coconut chips to cover the top completely, then press them lightly into the batter. Bake for an hour, then turn down the heat to 350°F, turn the pan around, and bake for a further 20 minutes, or until a skewer inserted comes out clean.

Take out of the oven and leave to cool completely in the pan. Brush off any scorched coconut flakes, cut into generous slices, and serve.

SALTED MISO BROWNIES

SALTED MISO BROWNIES

If I were in charge of brownies and their taxonomy (which, sadly, I'm not), there would be a proper list of categories. The only thing that unifies them really is the chocolate, beyond which they can be cakey, crumbly, chewy, or cocoa-y (and many other things beyond those beginning with the letter "c").

This one is my perfect brownie: dense and fudgy thanks to the chia seeds; rich, but not sickeningly so; with a salted caramel-like flavor that comes from using white miso and salt together. It makes this brownie incredibly special. And there is no category for that.

note / Use dark chocolate suitable for vegans if vegan.

Makes 16 brownies /

¼ cup + 1 tbsp ground chia seeds

½ cup + 2 tbsp (10 tbsp) refined coconut oil

9 oz dark chocolate (70%), broken into small pieces

1¾ cups light brown sugar

1 cup all-purpose flour

3 tbsp white miso

¾ tsp flaky sea salt

Preheat the oven to 400°F and line an 8-inch x 8-inch cake pan with parchment paper. In a small bowl, mix the ground chia seeds with 1 cup + 2 tbsp of water and set aside.

Place the coconut oil and broken chocolate in a medium-sized saucepan and set over a low heat. Stir occasionally until melted, then take off the heat. Mix in the sugar, flour, and miso, and crumble in the salt flakes. Finally, add the bloomed chia seeds and mix. Pour into the lined pan and gently shake to distribute the mixture.

Place on the middle shelf of the oven for 45 minutes or until firm to the touch around the edges with a slight wobble in the middle, then remove. The brownies might be wobbly in the middle, but they will soon settle down and become deliciously fudgy. Leave to cool completely, then cut into 16 squares.

See photos on previous pages

MILLI'S MATCHA ROLL CAKE
with raspberries and cream

Milli Taylor's grandma was Japanese. I assumed that she must have acquired her fantastic matcha baking skills from her, but sadly not. When her grandmother came to the UK in 1954, she didn't know any other Japanese people and as neither her husband nor her friends would contemplate eating bean curd, or seaweed, she had no option but to cook English food. Milli is now one of the best caterers in London. She might not have inherited her grandmother's recipes but she did inherit her Japanese love for perfection, and I count myself lucky to have borrowed this wonderful recipe.

note / You'll need a jelly roll pan (a shallow pan with a small lip) as close in size to 10 inches x 14 inches as you can find. If your pan is a little smaller, it will still work but your swirl might not be quite as satisfying. You'll also need an electric hand mixer.

Serves 9–10 /

¾ cup + 1 tbsp all-purpose flour

2 tbsp matcha powder

1 tsp baking powder

a pinch of salt

4 extra-large, fridge-cold eggs

½ cup + 2 tbsp superfine sugar

½ cup raspberry jam

Scant 1 cup heavy cream

2½ tbsp powdered sugar

Heaping ½ cup fresh raspberries

Preheat the oven to 400°F. Line your jelly roll pan with parchment paper, folding it tightly into the corners so the paper comes up the sides of the tray by 1 inch.

Sift together the flour, matcha, baking powder, and salt. Separate the whites of the eggs from the yolks into two large clean bowls, and add the superfine sugar to the yolks. Using an electric hand mixer, whisk the egg whites until they form stiff peaks. Without cleaning the whisk, move on to the next bowl and whisk the yolks and superfine sugar together for a couple of minutes until they double in volume, then stir the matcha flour mixture into the egg yolk bowl.

Using a large spatula, fold the egg whites into the yolks, being careful not to knock out too much air. Pour the batter into the lined pan and use a spatula to level the top. Tap the pan to release any air bubbles, then bake for 10 minutes, or until the sponge springs back to the touch.

Take the cake out of the oven and leave to rest for exactly 1 minute, then place a sheet of parchment paper over the top of the cake, followed by a large chopping board. Using oven gloves, turn the cake over and gently remove the pan. Carefully peel off the now top piece of parchment paper and replace with a new sheet just slightly larger

»

than the cake. Gently turn the cake back over again and pop it back into the pan.

Take a sharp knife and, at one of the short ends of the cake, score a mark ¾ of an inch in, all the way along the width of the cake. Tuck that end of parchment over that edge of the cake and begin to loosely roll the sponge from one short end to the other, rolling the parchment with it. Transfer your roll to a cooling rack with the seam on the bottom. Loosely cover with a clean kitchen towel and leave to cool for 30 minutes.

When the cake is cool, carefully unroll it and spread the jam over the sponge, right to the edges. Whisk the heavy cream and the powdered sugar together until you have soft peaks, then, leaving a ¾-inch border all around the sides, spread the cream on top of the jam so it is ½-inch thick. Scatter over the raspberries and gently press them into the cream. Roll the sponge back up again tightly (but without squeezing out the cream). With the seam on the bottom, place on a sheet pan and transfer to the fridge for a couple of hours to set.

When you're ready to serve the cake, remove from the fridge and, with a sharp knife, cut the roll into 9 to 10 even slices. This cake will keep in the fridge for two days, but it is best eaten on the day you make it.

DORAYAKI PANCAKES
with blueberry cream

The Portuguese have introduced a love of baking into many countries. In Sri Lanka there is the love cake; in Goa, India, the layered bebinca; and in Japan, the castella. Castella cake—a type of honey sponge—was brought over in the sixteenth century by Portuguese merchants to Nagasaki, where it is still a specialty today. It was adapted into the dorayaki: two soft, cake-like pancakes, sandwiched together with a filling in the middle. Here I've used a thick, cold blueberry cream as the filling, but if you don't have time to make the cream, mix a couple of tablespoons of your favorite jam into mascarpone instead.

note / The pancakes can brown quite easily, but there's ample batter here for you to test a couple of pancakes first for heat and size. Cook's perk.

Makes 6 sandwiches (12 pancakes) /

For the blueberry cream /
½ lb blueberries
1½ tsp lemon juice
¼ cup + 1 tsp superfine sugar
1 cup (16 tbsp) mascarpone cheese

For the pancakes /
1¼ cups all-purpose flour
¾ tsp baking powder
⅓ cup superfine sugar
2 eggs
1 tbsp clear honey
⅓ cup + 1 tbsp whole milk
canola oil

First make the blueberry cream. Place the blueberries in a small saucepan and mash lightly with a potato masher. Add a tablespoon of water, the lemon juice, and sugar, and place over a low heat. Cook for around 10 minutes, stirring regularly, until very sticky and all the moisture has evaporated. When you run a spoon across the bottom of the pan, there should be no liquid running from one side to the other. Transfer to a heatproof bowl to cool for 10 minutes, then combine with the mascarpone and place in the fridge.

To make the pancakes, mix all the dry ingredients together in a bowl. In a jug, mix the eggs, honey, and milk together, then pour into the dry ingredients. Stir well until there are no lumps in the batter. Place a non-stick frying pan over a medium heat, wipe a little oil around the pan with a paper towel, and, when hot, drop 2 tablespoons of batter into the pan. Cook for 2 minutes, until the surface of the pancake has a lot of bubbles and the edges are dry, then flip over and cook for 30 seconds to a minute more. Transfer to a plate, and repeat until you have 12 pancakes.

To assemble the dorayaki, spread some blueberry cream on one pancake and place another pancake on top and lightly press down. Use the back of a spoon or a knife to smooth the edges of the cream if you wish, then press down the sides to seal, and serve.

BANANA TARTE TATIN
with cinnamon, black pepper, and cloves

The tarte tatin is a design classic. Here I have adapted it using bananas and a small amount of cinnamon, black pepper, and cloves. The key to turning out the tarte tatin is to be prepared: before you put it in the oven, choose a plate to turn it out onto which is larger than your pan—and don't compromise on the oven glove-wear.

note / You'll need a 12-inch ovenproof frying pan or tatin pan for this recipe.

Serves 4 /

¾ cup light brown sugar

½ tsp ground cinnamon

a pinch of ground cloves

⅛ tsp finely ground black pepper

5 small to medium bananas, peeled and cut in half lengthways

all-purpose flour, for dusting

1 x 14-oz puff pastry sheet, defrosted

Preheat the oven to 400°F and keep your ovenproof frying pan or tatin pan within reach.

Place the sugar in a small saucepan and add 2 tablespoons of water. Mix with your fingertips and pat into a single layer. Place the saucepan over a high heat and allow the sugar to bubble and dissolve for around 3 minutes, then remove from the heat and add the cinnamon, cloves, and pepper. Stir, then pour into your ovenproof frying pan or tatin pan.

Place the halved bananas closely together in the frying pan or tatin pan, cut side down, to make a fan shape. Fill any gaps with more cut banana if need be. Flour your work surface, then roll out the puff pastry until it's just bigger than the top of the pan (around 13 inches) and the thickness of a quarter. Drape the pastry over your rolling pin, carefully lay it over the pan, and gently tuck down the edges around the bananas, making sure there are no gaps. Prick the pastry all over with a fork (to ensure the steam escapes and the pastry will crisp) and place in the oven for 30 minutes, or until golden brown.

Make sure you're wearing padded oven gloves on both hands when you remove the tarte tatin from the oven, as the caramel will be volcano hot. You need to turn the tarte tatin out immediately, so take extra care. Once it's out of the oven, place a large plate (larger than the size of the pan) over the top of the pan and gently turn it over, shaking gently, then remove the pan carefully.

Serve still warm. It goes very well with a little creme fraiche or yogurt sweetened with powdered sugar and brightened with a little lime juice.

ROSE STRAWBERRIES with strained saffron yogurt

The riper and sweeter the strawberries you buy, the better this simple and elegant dish will taste, but given that those strawberries would be lovely on their own, perhaps here you should use those that haven't quite managed to reach their full potential. Both components (strawberries and strained yogurt) can be made in advance, leaving you to pull off some effortless-looking hosting if people are coming around for dinner. My only word of advice is to determine whether you have rose water, or rose essence or extract made using alcohol. If you have the latter, add it drop by drop and into a spoon first, so you don't accidentally pour the whole thing in (like I once did).

note / You'll need to start this the morning ahead of lunch, or at lunch for dinner. You'll also need cheesecloth or a clean kitchen towel and a sieve to make the strained yogurt.

Serves 4 /

For the strained saffron yogurt /

35 oz Greek yogurt

12 strands of saffron

¾ tsp ground cardamom or ground seeds of 4–5 pods

½ cup + 1 tbsp powdered sugar

For the strawberries /

1 lb strawberries, leaves removed, quartered

⅓ cup powdered sugar

1 tsp rose water (if an extract like Nielsen-Massey, use scant ¼ tsp)

1 tbsp lemon juice

To make the strained saffron yogurt, line a sieve with cheesecloth or a kitchen towel, place over a deep bowl, and pour in the yogurt. Scoop up all four corners of the cheesecloth, tie them together, and place the sieve and the bowl in the fridge for at least 4 hours. When it's done, the yogurt should be fairly stiff with at least a few tablespoons of liquid in the bottom of the bowl. How much you end up with will depend on the type of yogurt and how much whey there is in it, but you should have around 19 oz; if you have a lot more, pop the extra in the fridge for later.

When you're happy with the texture of the strained yogurt, place the saffron in a small bowl with 1 teaspoon of freshly boiled water and leave to soften for a minute. Add the saffron and its water, the cardamom, and sugar to the strained yogurt and mix well.

To marinate the strawberries, place them in a bowl with the sugar, rose water, and lemon juice. Gently stir, and pop into the fridge for at least an hour.

To serve, divide the yogurt between four shallow bowls, then spoon over the strawberries and some of their juice.

helpful things

INGREDIENTS

Bird's-eye chiles

Once bitten, never forgotten. These tiny red or green chiles, sometimes called "Thai chiles," send a lightning bolt of heat through anything they touch. Their heat is often tempered in Thai and Vietnamese dishes with salt, sugar, vinegar, and/or coconut milk. They are widely available in supermarkets and can be frozen whole.

Bok choy

This is a type of Chinese cabbage, and with its tender green leaves and juicy white bulb it's unlike any English cabbages. Most people halve them, but I like to shred them lengthways to get a little leaf and juice in each bite. They can be boiled, fried, or steamed in a matter of minutes and are available widely in supermarkets.

Chile bean sauce (toban djan)

Made using fermented fava beans and chiles, which give the resulting dish a good level of heat and funk. This is a critical ingredient in mapo tofu (see page 171). Lee Kum Kee, a popular brand, is sold in larger supermarkets and online.

Chinkiang vinegar

This sharp black vinegar is brewed from glutinous rice and is the perfect antidote to anything rich, as it slices through it like a freshly sharpened knife. It's used in dipping sauces and is available in most Asian supermarkets. If you can't find it, a cheap, sharp balsamic is a good substitute and, failing that, white wine vinegar—but it won't have the same edge.

Choy sum

This leggy green vegetable has a long juicy stem and large tender leaves. You can shred the leaves, cut the stalk, and cook them both together. It's less bulbous than bok choy, and is available all year round.

Coconut milk

Coconut milk varies so much. In my opinion, the best in class are the Thai brands Chaokoh and Aroy-D, because they contain over 50 percent extracted coconut, they have few or no preservatives, and they don't tend to split as much as some other brands.

Galangal

Like ginger, galangal is a rhizome, but unlike ginger, it tastes citrusy and pine-y. It can be found in Asian supermarkets.

Gochujang

This Korean red pepper paste is a spicy, sticky, and sweet condiment of joy. It's often made using chiles, glutinous rice, fermented soy beans, and sugar. I love it in Korean bibimbap (see page 148), kimchi fried rice (see page 136), or just slathered over vegetables and roasted, as in my roasted carrots and cabbage (see page 238). It has a long shelf life and is found in Asian supermarkets and some chain supermarkets.

Green finger chiles

These are the standard-issue chiles in India. Slim and green, their heat is bright, fresh, and not ear-ticklingly hot, so they're sometimes used in addition to Kashmiri chile powder. Available in Indian markets. If you can't find these, substitute serrano chiles.

Hoisin sauce

The darling of the Chinese sauce world, this sauce is built to please anyone and anything it touches. Made using fermented soybeans, garlic, sesame, sugar, and spice, it can be bought in most supermarkets.

Kashmiri chile powder

This is my favorite chile powder because it's mild-mannered and colorful. A little will give a rounded gentle warmth to a dish. Add it by the ½ teaspoon until your dish tastes just right to you. My preferred brand is Fudco, which is available online. If you can't find this, substitute a mild red chile powder.

Kecap manis

An Indonesian condiment, often called "sweet soy." It's made using fermented soybeans but it's thicker, sweeter, and more syrupy than soy sauce. You can buy it in Asian supermarkets or online, or make something similar at home (see page 256).

Kimchi

This is Korea's gift to the world: hot salted and fermented vegetables, predominantly cabbage, but often carrot, daikon, ginger, and garlic. It can be bought in sealed vac packs or in jars in larger supermarkets or online. The jarred kimchi is often fresher with a richer, more developed flavor but you will need to "burp" it every now and again by loosening the lid to release some of the pressure build-up.

Kombu

A type of thick, flat seaweed cultivated in the northern waters of Japan and Korea. Steeped in hot water, it makes for a delicious umami-rich stock. It's available in Asian supermarkets and online.

Makrut lime leaves

These glossy leaves add a citrus-floral meets tropical-forest fragrance to dishes. They can be bought fresh in certain supermarkets, frozen in Asian supermarkets—but if you can't find either fresh or frozen, then dried are available online. Crush them to release their oils, leave them to infuse into dishes, and fish them out just before serving.

Mirin

This sweet rice wine is used in Japanese cooking, and is not to be confused with rice vinegar. It gives dishes sweetness primarily, but also depth of flavor, and is often used to balance the saltiness of soy sauce.

Salted fermented black beans

These tiny little black beans are like olives or anchovies in the intensity of their salt and umami. They're used as they are in mapo tofu (see page 171), or to make black bean paste. Both the Zheng Feng and Koon Chun brands can be found in most Asian supermarkets in a bag under the name "salted black beans."

Sichuan peppercorns

This very special and unusual pepper smells of grapefruit, and though it isn't very hot it will make your tongue tingle and numb it gently and briefly.

Soy sauce

Soy sauces like Kikkoman are clean, crisp, thin, and salty: perfect to add umami-rich flavors and salt to dishes—this is the type I use most widely, to allow other flavors to shine through. Dark soy is thicker and richer, with a molasses-like flavor. Tamari can be used as a substitute for either.

Sriracha

A wonderful hot sauce of Thai origin in which heat, sweetness, and salt are balanced in equal measure. I like to drizzle this over my eggs in the morning, but it can be used as a secret weapon to add punch to many dishes. Available widely in supermarkets.

Thai basil

Also known as Thai "sweet basil," this Thai herb tastes sweet and aniseedy and is often added to curries and stir-fries toward the end of cooking so that its fragrance isn't destroyed by heat. It's quite delicate and won't last long, so keep it in the fridge and use it as soon as you can. You can find it in some supermarkets and in Asian markets.

Toasted sesame oil

Toasted sesame oil is not generally used for cooking with heat, as its flavor deteriorates on contact: it's much better used as a seasoning. It's widely available in most supermarkets.

ONLINE SUPPLIERS

General

For East and South East Asian ingredients
99 Ranch is a nationwide pan-Asian grocery store chain. www.99ranch.com

For South Asian ingredients
Kalustyan's is a New York–based grocery store that ships nationwide and stocks everything from date syrup and rosewater to moong dal and dried fenugreek. www.foodsofnations.com

Specialists

Korean specialists
Get your kimchi, gochujang, and K-Pop from one store: www.hmart.com

Indian specialists
For curry leaves, Indian red chile powder, and all the dal your heart could desire, visit www.ishopindian.com

Thai specialists
For galangal, Thai basil, and Makrut lime leaves: www.grocerythai.com

For spices
This store stocks single-origin spices with a more transparent supply chain than what you buy in the supermarket. www.oaktownspiceshop.com

For flours and vegan baking ingredients
Ingredients like fine semolina, almond flour, and ground flaxseeds are all available from Bob's Red Mill. www.bobsredmill.com

FURTHER READING

These food writers and books have all helped me to add new ingredients, techniques, and, in some cases, cuisines to my kitchen:

Alford, Jeffrey, and Naomi Duguid, *Hot Sour Salty Sweet* (Artisan, 2000)

Anderson, Tim, *Nanban* (Clarkson Potter, 2016); and *JapanEasy* (Hardie Grant Books, 2017)

Bourke, Jordan, and Rejina Pyo, *Our Korean Kitchen* (Weldon Owen, 2017)

Chang, David, and Peter Meehan, *Momofuku* (Clarkson Potter, 2009)

Duguid, Naomi, *Burma* (Artisan, 2012)

Dunlop, Fuchsia, *Sichuan Cookery* (Gardners Books, 2003); *Shark's Fin and Sichuan Pepper: A Sweet-Sour Memoir of Eating in China* (W. W. Norton & Company, 2009); *Every Grain of Rice: Simple Chinese Home Cooking* (W. W. Norton & Company, 2013)

Ford, Eleanor, *Fire Islands: Recipes from Indonesia* (Apollo Publishers, 2019)

Hachisu, Nancy Singleton, *Japanese Farm Food* (Andrews McMeel Publishing, 2012)

Jaffrey, Madhur, *Madhur Jaffrey's World-of-the-East Vegetarian Cooking* (Knopf, 1981); *Indian Cooking* (B.E.S. Publishing, 2003); *Ultimate Curry Bible* (Ebury Press, 2003)

Kuruvita, Peter, *Serendip: My Sri Lankan Kitchen* (Murdoch Books, 2009)

Meehan, Peter, *Lucky Peach Presents 101 Easy Asian Recipes* (Clarkson Potter, 2015)

Nguyen, Andrea, *Asian Tofu* (Ten Speed Press, 2012)

Owen, Sri, *Indonesian Food* (Pavillion Books, 2015)

Solomon, Charmaine, *The Complete Asian Cookbook* (Hardie Grant Books, 2017)

Thompson, David, *Thai Food* (Ten Speed Press, 2002)

THANK YOU

Books are not built by a single hand but by many. Thank you goes out to every person who's written a production schedule for *East*, sat in a sales meeting, proofread, indexed, designed, recommended a place to eat, or tweaked a piece of cilantro at a photo shoot—they are all responsible for what you hold in your hands.

With extra-special thanks:

To the Guardians

To **Melissa Denes**: without you this book wouldn't exist. Thank you for the opportunity you gave me to write in the *Guardian* and thereby grow, learn, and write recipes for more people.

To **Bob Granleese**, for being a great editor, and **Tim Lusher**, for your boundless enthusiasm.

To the behind-the-scenes team: art director **Bruno Haward**, photographer **Louise Hagger**; prop stylist **Jen Kay** and food stylist **Emily Kydd**—thanks for keeping my recipes in the *Guardian* looking sharp.

To the Penguins

To **Juliet Annan**, my editor and publisher in the UK: your shrieks of excitement about the food I cook and write about make me want to write more books for you. Thank you for your unwavering support and dedication to making every book we work on together brilliant.

To **John Hamilton**: thank you for your creativity and the energy, passion, and the love you poured into this book. I am so happy we were able to make this book together.

To **Sarah Fraser**: for your care and beautiful design—thank you.

To **David Loftus**: thanks for bringing along your best camera and your stories but also for capturing food and life in a way no one else ever could.

To the rest of the team: **David Ettridge** and **Assallah Tahir** for help in all areas; **Poppy North** and **Sapphire Rees** for press; **Samantha Fanaken** and **Ben Hughes** for helping to sell the book; **Caroline Pretty** for your astute copy-editing; **Caroline Wilding** for indexing; **Emma Brown**, **Gail Jones**, **Annie Underwood**, and **Rose Poole**, thank you.

To the Flatiron team

To **Will Schwalbe**, my American editor, and all the team at Flatiron Books—including **Andrea Mosqueda** and **Emily Walters**—for your wonderful effervescence and for believing in my work enough to take it transatlantic (and for being so brilliant to work with). To **Sarah Chamberlain**, for so diligently translating all the grams to cups, kilos to pounds, and coriander to cilantro—thank you. And many thanks to **Kim Yorio** and **Aimee Bianca** from YCM Media for helping the book to take flight.

To the agents

To my special agents, **Jane Finigan** and **Felicity Rubinstein**, for being the best representatives, advisers, and friends an author could have.

To my team

To **Ben Benton**, cook extraordinaire and my right-hand man. Thanks for your talent, which comes so easily, your friendship, and for making me laugh to the point I'd be able to season a dish with my tears.

To **Henrietta Inman**, pastry chef, for your friendship and wisdom in helping me to navigate baking without eggs, milk, and butter. But also for the edible treats along the way.

To **Hannah Rose Cameron McKenna** and **Trishna Shah** for testing every recipe, and for finessing, tightening, and polishing every single one so they work reliably for others.

To **Georgia Levy**, for such grace under pressure when styling shoots, and **Jen Kay**, for again finding the most beautiful plates, bowls, and other props for the shoots.

To my family and friends

To **Meron** and **Fanus**, for making Arya so happy and supporting me in many hours of need, and to **Gen, Giulia, and team**, for keeping Lola's tail wagging.

To **Diana Henry** and **James Thompson**: thank you for telling me to keep going when I didn't think I could. Very much appreciated.

To my parents and in-laws, **Mum** and **Dad**, **Barbara** and **Kevin**, **Peter** and **Roubina**, for all the love, encouragement, and extra arms.

Most of all, thank you to **Hugh**, for being the finest example of a human being known to exist. Thank you for your help and support but most of all for your gigantic love and this life we have together, filled with our sweet small things, adventure, laughter (and good food).

INDEX

www.flatironbooks.com

Photography copyright © David Loftus, 2019
Illustrations copyright © Monika Forsberg, 2019
JH Hare by Gray318

The Library of Congress Cataloging-in-Publication Data is available upon request.

ISBN 978-1-250-75073-0 (paper over board)
ISBN 978-1-250-75074-7 (ebook)

Our books may be purchased in bulk for promotional, educational, or business use. Please contact your local bookseller or the Macmillan Corporate and Premium Sales Department at 1-800-221-7945, extension 5442, or by email at MacmillanSpecialMarkets@macmillan.com.

Originally published in Great Britain by Fig Tree, an imprint of Penguin Random House, UK

First U.S. Edition: 2020

10 9 8 7 6 5 4 3